INTERMEDIATE

BLUES GUITAR

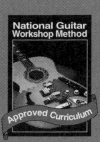

The Complete Electric Blues Guitar Method

Beginning · Intermediate · Mastering

MATT SMITH

Alfred, the leader in educational publishing, and the National Guitar Workshop, one of America's finest guitar schools, have joined forces to bring you the best, most progressive educational tools possible. We hope you will enjoy this book and encourage you to look for other fine products from Alfred and the National Guitar Workshop.

Acquisition and editorial: Nathaniel Gunod, Workshop Arts
Music typesetting and interior design: Miriam Davidson, Workshop Arts
Chord and scale illustrations: David Jacobs
Recording engineered and produced by Mark Dzuiba, Workshop Sounds, High Falls, New York
Cover photo: Jeff Oshiro • Cover design: Ted Engelbart/Carol Kascsak
Cover model: David White • Guitar courtesy of Fender Musical Instruments Corp.

TABLE OF CONTENTS

ABOUT THE AUTHOR

Matt Smith has been playing guitar for over twenty years. He teaches privately and spends his summers teaching advanced rock and blues guitar at the National Guitar Summer Workshop's Connecticut campus. Band leader/guitarist/lead singer of the Matt Smith Band, Matt has been called on stage by the likes of Al DiMeola, Tinsley Ellis, Greg Allman, Andy Timmons, Toy Caldwell and Rik Emmett. He is a featured monthly columnist for *Guitar for the Practicing Musician*, as well as a nationally renowned endorsee/clinician for Ovation, Takamine and Hamer Guitars and Trace Elliot amplifiers. Matt Smith has written two other books, the *Bending* and *Speed* Guitar Technique Builders, also published by the National Guitar Workshop and Alfred.

"Smith sweeps a broad spectrum of emotions in a panorama that takes your breath away like watching a sunset kiss a mountain range before slipping into the sea."
Don Wilcox,
Troy Record

"Matt Smith will lead the pack of guitarists in the 90's."
Seth Kaufman
Buzz Magazine

The Matt Smith Band took first place in the prestigious Tanqueray Rocks contest, defeating over 1200 bands in a nationwide search. This resulted in the Tanqueray Rock 1—Live at the Ritz CD, which is distributed nationally by Tower Records. The band was also named Best Rock Band-1991 in the Metroland Magazine reader's poll. Matt and his band have performed with B.B. King, Spin Doctors, Jeff Healy, Buddy Guy, Johnny Winter, Tower of Power, Robben Ford, Delbert McClinton, Warren Zevon and others.

INTRODUCTION

The blues have been an important part of my life since I was just a kid. There is something so compelling, so timeless about this soulful music that no matter what style I explore on the guitar, I always come home to the blues!

Every guitarist, regardless of experience or style, can learn from this great American art form. The blues are the roots of all jazz and rock music. It is a music that is constantly evolving into new forms with the input of each new generation of musicians.

This series of books is designed to be easily understood by the self-taught guitarist as well as the schooled student. The *Intermediate* method is aimed at players of some experience, as well as more advanced guitarists that wish to brush up on the basics.

My book is the result of some twenty-odd years of living, singing and playing the blues. I hope you enjoy it as much as I did writing it for you!

This book is dedicated to my students, all the staff at the National Guitar Summer Workshop, my friends at Kaman Music and *Guitar for the Practicing Musician Magazine*, and Julian Porter, whose gracious help made this book possible.

000
Track
00.0

An audio recording is available for every book in this series. We hope it will make learning with these books easier and more enjoyable. This symbol will appear next to every example that is played on the audio recording. Use the recording—and your rewind button!— to help insure that you are capturing the feel of each example, interpreting the rhythms correctly, and so on. If you have the compact disc version of this book, you can use the Track numbers below the symbol to go directly to the examples for any page. Have fun!

CHAPTER 1

Getting Started

The first part of this book is here as a review. If you know the guitar fingerboard, how to tune, are a wiz at reading standard music notation, TAB, scale and chord diagrams and Roman numerals, you can skip ahead to the next chapter.

THE MUSICAL ALPHABET

OK, lets talk numbers! Being a self-taught musician, music theory used to scare the heck out of me. Then one day I realized that music is really just like basic arithmetic. **Just remember that a *whole step* equals a distance of two frets on your guitar, and a *half step* equals a distance of one fret.** All notes are separated by either a whole step or a half step. Natural notes with a whole step, or two frets between them are: A-B, C-D, D-E, F-G and G-A. The notes with a half step, or one fret between them are B-C and E-F.

Notes:	A		B		C		D		E		F		G		A
Steps:		W		H		W		W		H		W		W	

> **W** = Whole Step
> **H** = Half Step

Notes that are a whole step apart have a *chromatic* note in between: a *sharp* ♯, or a *flat* ♭. Notice that chromatic notes can have two names. For instance, C♯ and D♭ fall on the same fret and sound the same. These are called *enharmonic equivalents*. Don't worry! We'll go into this more thoroughly later.

THE GUITAR FINGERBOARD

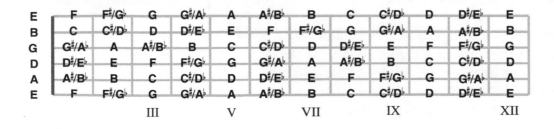

Get the idea? GREAT! Now let's review more of the basics.

TUNING

Over the course of hundreds of years, the guitar has been tuned in many ways. The tuning that we refer to today as *standard tuning* is one of a myriad of possible tunings. Standard tuning has evolved as a good compromise that makes chord forms manageable and retains some of the characteristics of so called "open tunings." There are many methods used by musicians to tune their guitar properly. Most of you have probably tuned by comparing the fifth fret of one string to the next higher open string (fourth fret in the case of the G to the B string).

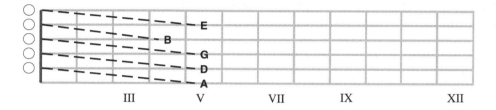

TUNING WITH HARMONICS

Many people prefer to tune with *harmonics*. A harmonic is the bell-like tone produced by lightly touching a vibrating string at precise points (*nodes*) along its length. On the guitar the primary natural harmonics are found at the twelfth, seventh, and fifth frets. Touch the string directly above the fret wire itself without pushing down.

Using harmonics: **Tune 4th string 7th fret to A 440 (see below)**
Tune 5th string 5th fret to 4th string 7th fret
Tune 6th string 5th fret to 5th string 7th fret
Tune 3rd string 7th fret to 4th string 5th fret
Tune 2nd string open to 6th string 7th fret
Tune 1st string open to 6th string 5th fret
(no fretted notes are used)

Tune the sixth string carefully, since it is used to tune the first and second strings. Of course, comparison tuning can be done without starting at A 440, or *concert pitch,* but most musicians tune to that pitch.

Tuning for a beginner or any guitar player can be greatly simplified by using an **electronic tuner.** It is important, however, to train your ear so that you can hear and tune properly. Any musician must be able to hear when their instrument is out of tune.

A 440, or concert pitch, can be obtained from a tuning fork or other fixed-pitch instrument (e.g. piano).

Learning to read music will help you to get the most out of your National Guitar Workshop and Alfred instructional books. It will make you a better musician, too, because you will be able to communicate more easily with other musicians. What follows is a discussion of music reading basics. Remember that practice makes perfect! The more you practice reading, the easier it will become.

PITCH

Staff: A *staff* containing five lines and four spaces is used to write music. Notes are alternately written on the lines and spaces in alphabetical order.

Clef: The *clef* indicates which notes coincide with a particular line or space. Different clefs are used for different instruments. Guitar music is written in G clef. The inside curl of the G clef encircles the line which will be called "G." When the G clef is placed on the second line, as it is in guitar music, it is called the *treble clef.*

Using the G clef the notes are as follows*:

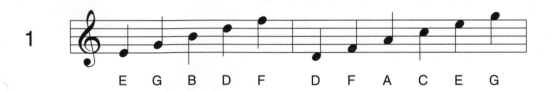

Ledger lines: These are lines that are used to indicate pitch above and below the staff.

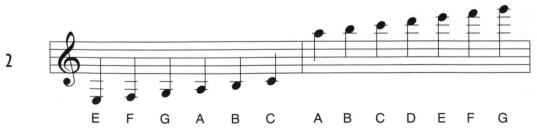

* In standard notation the guitar sounds an octave lower than written.

TIME

Measure: The staff is divided by vertical lines called *bar lines*. The space between two bar lines is called a *measure*. Each measure (bar) is an equal unit of time.

3

Time Signature: Every piece of music has numbers at the beginning that tell us how to count the time.

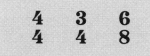

The top number represents the number of beats or counts per measure. The bottom number represents the type of note receiving one count. For example: 4 = quarter note, and 8 = eighth note. Sometimes a **C** is written in place of 4/4 time. This is called *common time*.

Note values in 4/4 time:

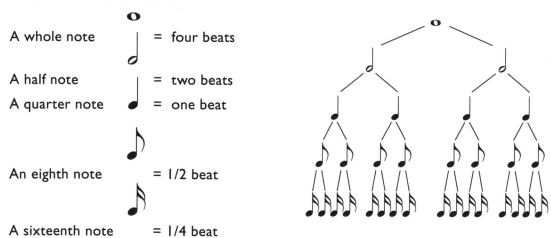

A whole note = four beats

A half note = two beats

A quarter note = one beat

An eighth note = 1/2 beat

A sixteenth note = 1/4 beat

Rests: For every note value, there is a corresponding *rest*. Rests indicate silence in music.

4

Whole Note Rest   Half Note Rest   Quarter Note Rest   Eighth Note Rest   Sixteenth Note Rest

RHYTHMIC NOTATION

Another type of notation used frequently in guitar music is called *rhythmic notation*. It is a system of slash marks and beams that notate specific rhythms without specific pitch. This notation is usually used to indicate the rhythm to be played for the chord written above the staff. The notation is similar to standard notation.

Counting syllables are used to describe parts of a beat. When we break a beat in half we use numbers for the first half and a "+" sign for the second half. When we sub-divide beats into four parts we use an "e" for the second part and an "a" for the fourth, for example, 1 e + a (said one-ee-and-ah).

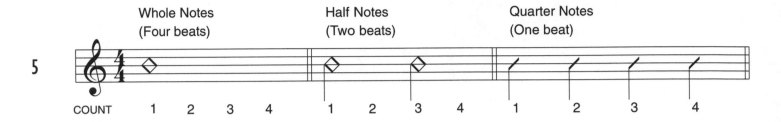

A dot increases the length of a note by one half of its original value.

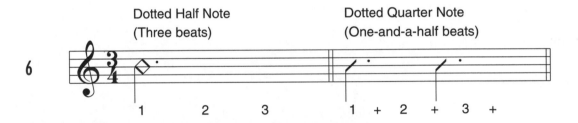

Connecting notes that are less than one beat in duration is called *beaming*.

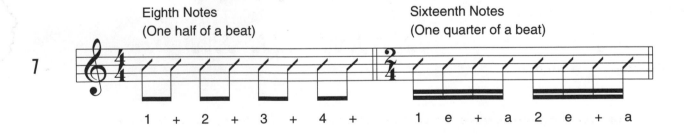

Tied Notes

When notes are *tied*, the second note is not struck but its time value is added to the first.

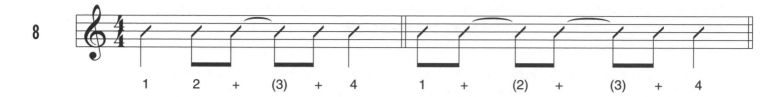

8

1   2   +   (3)   +   4   1   +   (2)   +   (3)   +   4

Triplets

A group of three notes that divide the beat(s) into three equal parts.

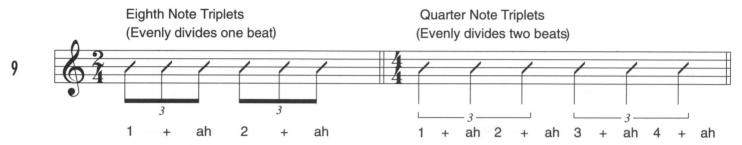

Eighth Note Triplets
(Evenly divides one beat)

Quarter Note Triplets
(Evenly divides two beats)

9

1   +   ah   2   +   ah   1   +   ah   2   +   ah   3   +   ah   4   +   ah

Notice that to count quarter note triplets, you can still count "1 and ah 2 and ah" as with eighth note triplets. The difference is that each triplet quarter note is worth two triplet eighth notes.

B.B. King

PHOTO • Cesar Vera/Courtesy of MCA

A GUIDE TO TABLATURE

Tablature, when combined with standard music notation, provides the most complete system for communicating the many possibilities in guitar playing.

In our TAB system, as in most, *rhythm* is not notated. For that, you will have to refer to the standard notation. Six lines are used to indicate the six strings of the guitar. The top line is the high E string (the string closest to the floor) and the bottom line is the low E string. Numbers are placed on the strings to indicate frets. If there is a "0," play that string open.

Fingerings are often included in TAB. You will find them just under the bottom line. A "1" indicates your left first (or index) finger. A "4" indicates your left fourth or pinky finger.

In the following example, the first note is played with the first finger on the first fret. The next note is played with the second finger on the second fret, then third finger plays the third fret, and the fourth finger plays the fourth fret.

A **tie** in the music is indicated in TAB by placing the tied note in parentheses.

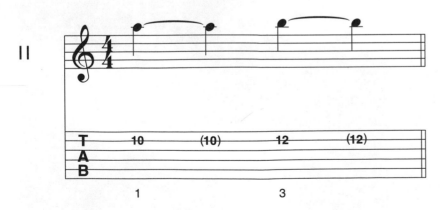

Hammer-ons and pull-offs are indicated with slur marks, just like in standard notation. Our TAB also includes an "H" for hammer-ons and a "P" for pull-offs. These are found just above the TAB.

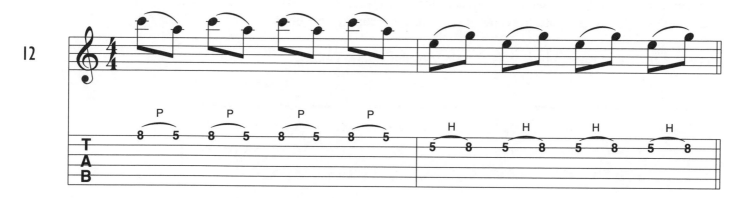

Upward **bends** are marked with upward **arrows**. Downward arrows are used to show a reverse bend. A number above the arrow indicates how far to bend (1 = a whole step, 1/2 = a half step, etc.). Remember that the TAB will show the fret number on which your finger should be placed. The standard music notation shows the actual resulting sound. Notice that the small grace note in the standard notation corresponds with the fret shown in the TAB. In the following example you will also find a **slide** (S above ⟋) and a **tap** (T). Also, notice that reverse bends appear in parentheses in the TAB. Some notes are actually represented by the arrows themselves, as in the second note of the triplet in this example.

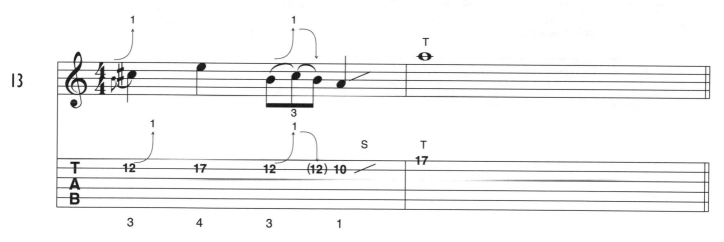

In the following example you will find several more symbols: the signs for **picking** down (⊓), the sign for picking up (V) and the sign for **vibrato** (⟳⟳).

ROMAN NUMERALS

Musicians traditionally use *Roman numerals* to indicate functional names of chords in a key. You will find this system used in some of the later chapters of this book.

Here is a review of Roman numerals and their Arabic equivalents:

I	1	IV	4	VII	7	X	10	XIII	13	XVI	16
II	2	V	5	VIII	8	XI	11	XIV	14	XVII	17
III	3	VI	6	IX	9	XII	12	XV	15		

Note that major chords are indicated with upper case Roman numerals, and that minor chords and diminished chords are in lower case numerals. *For more information about this see our book, Beginning Blues Guitar*, Chapter 2.

READING SCALE AND CHORD DIAGRAMS

Scales

This book is filled with scale diagrams. The top line represents the first string of the guitar, and the bottom line the sixth. The vertical lines represent frets, which are numbered with Roman numerals.

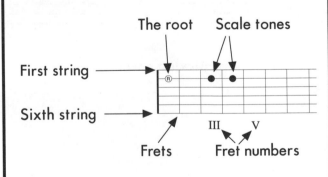

Chords

There are lots of chord diagrams to read as well. They are similar to the scale diagrams, except they are oriented vertically instead of horizontally. Vertical lines represent strings, and horizontal lines represent frets. Roman numerals are used to number the frets.

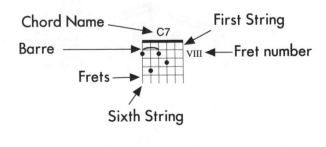

CHAPTER 2

Theory

A *scale* is a group, flock, herd or gaggle of notes separated by set distances. These distances are measured in whole and half steps. The most common scale is the *major* scale. When you hear musicians talking to each other in numbers, they are talking about notes as they relate to scales or chords.

THE MAJOR SCALE

There are seven notes in a major scale, with the eighth note being an *octave* above the first. An octave is the distance of twelve half steps or eight scale degrees, and involves two notes with the same name, only higher or lower in pitch. The first two notes in "Somewhere Over the Rainbow" are an octave apart.

A major scale can begin on any note. Sometimes the set distances used to create major scales will result in notes that are sharp or flat (but never both!). Confused? Look at the guitar fingerboard diagram on page 6. Observe the G on the third fret and the A on the fifth fret of the sixth (lowest) string. Notice the fret between them. The fourth fret has two names. It could be called G$\sharp$, if the G needed to be raised one half step, or it could be called A$\flat$ if the A needed to be lowered by a half step. Why would you want to do that? To make the notes fit into a scale! The first note in the scale gives the scale its name. This is the *key note*, *tonic* or *root* (R). Here is the formula for the major scale:

Scale degree:	R		2		3		4		5		6		7		8
Step:		W		W		H		W		W		W		H	

W = Whole step
H = Half step

As you now know, a major scale is a series of tones arranged in a specific pattern of whole and half steps. The letter names appear in alphabetical order. (Never use the same letter name twice in a row! This will save lots of confusion.) Together, these notes comprise the key. Here is the series of notes known as the C Major scale, which comprise the key of C Major.

C MAJOR SCALE

Notice that when you start on a C note, the natural half steps of E to F and B to C fall conveniently so that no sharps or flats are needed. When the root is a note other than C, certain notes in the scale will have to be altered to bring about the correct sequence of whole steps and half steps. Let's build a D Major scale so you can practice using the major scale formula.

1. Write out   **R   2   3   4   5   6   7   R**
                   W   W   H   W   W   W   H

2. Since D is the root of the scale, place a D over the R at the beginning and the end. Move up a whole step (two frets). You should find an E. Place E over the 2 on your scale.

3. We now need another whole step. Look again at the guitar fingerboard diagram on page 6 and move a whole step up (two frets) from E. You should now be on F♯. Place an F♯ over the 3.

4. Now its time for a half step! Look at the diagram and move up a half step (one fret) from F♯. You should find a G. Place a G over the 4. The next whole step in the diagram is an A. Place this over the 5 in your scale.

5. The next whole step should be a B. B should be 6 in your scale. The next whole step (two frets) up from B is C♯. Place this over the 7 in your scale.

6. One final half step (one fret) up from C♯ is D. This completes the scale. Here is how it looks:

             D   E   F♯   G   A   B   C♯   D
             R   2   3   4   5   6   7   R

Hopefully you can now write out a major scale. Practice writing out major scales starting on different roots.

D MAJOR SCALE

16

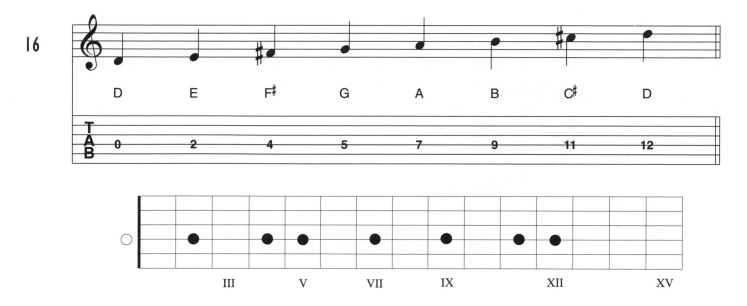

Here is an example of a major scale that results in the use of flats rather than sharps.

B♭ MAJOR SCALE

17

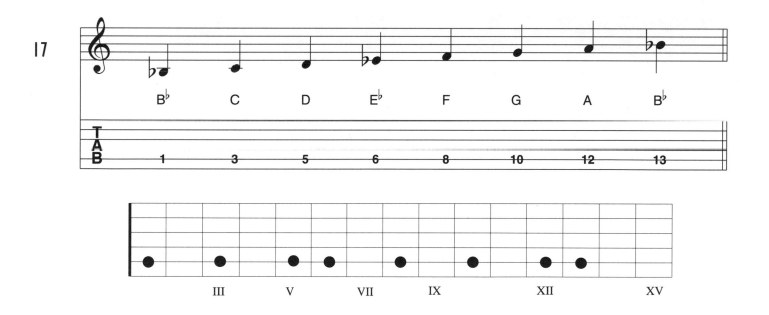

Using sharps and flats, it is possible to create a major scale from any note.

The Major Scales

1	2	3	4	5	6	7	8	
C	D	E	F	G	A	B	C	
G	A	B	C	D	E	F#	G	
D	E	F#	G	A	B	C#	D	
A	B	C#	D	E	F#	G#	A	
E	F#	G#	A	B	C#	D#	E	
B	C#	D#	E	F#	G#	A#	B	
F#	G#	A#	B	C#	D#	E#	F#	} Enharmonic*
G♭	A♭	B♭	C♭	D♭	E♭	F	G♭	
D♭	E♭	F	G♭	A♭	B♭	C	D♭	
A♭	B♭	C	D♭	E♭	F	G	A♭	
E♭	F	G	A♭	B♭	C	D	E♭	
B♭	C	D	E♭	F	G	A	B♭	
F	G	A	B♭	C	D	E	F	

*The F# and G♭ scales are actually all the same notes (enharmonically equivalent), so, including C Major, there are a total of twelve major scales.

KEY SIGNATURES

A key signature is a collection of all the flats or sharps that are used in a particular scale. It is placed at the beginning of a line of music to indicate what notes should always be sharped or flatted in that music, creating the sound of a particular *key*. For example, if you always sharp C and F, it will create an overall sound of the D Major scale, or the key of D.

The Twelve Key Signatures

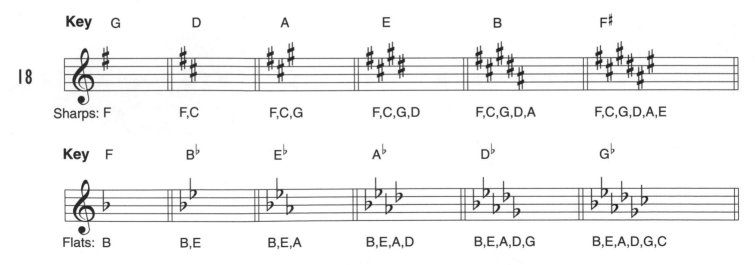

Sharps and flats take their names from the line or space on which they appear. Since a note on the top line of the staff would be an F, for instance, a sharp on that line would be an F sharp.

NATURAL MINOR SCALE

Minor scales are derived from major scales. For example, the A Minor scale is made up of the notes of the C Major scale played from A to A.

The minor scale, like the major scale, has a formula of whole steps and half steps, making it possible to create a minor scale starting from any note.

Notes:	A		B		C		D		E		F		G		A
Steps:		W		H		W		W		H		W		W	

Compared to an A Major scale, the 3rd, 6th and 7th degrees of A Minor are all a half step closer to the root of the scale. These degrees are said to be *flatted* or *minor* and are indicated with a flat sign (♭3, ♭6, ♭7).

RELATIVE MINOR

For every major key, there is a *relative minor key* which is built on the sixth tone of the major scale for the key. For instance, in the key of C, the note A is the sixth tone (C D E F G A), so A Minor is the relative minor key of C Major. The example below shows all the key signatures with their corresponding major and minor keys.

Key Signature	Major Key	Minor Key	Key Signature	Major Key	Minor Key
	C	A		F	D
	G	E		B♭	G
	D	B		E♭	C
	A	F♯		A♭	F
	E	C♯		D♭	B♭
	B	G♯		G♭	E♭
	F♯	D♯			

An interval is the distance between any two notes. In fact, the terms "whole steps" and "half steps" are just different ways to refer to major 2nd and minor 2nd intervals.

The example below indentifies the interval of each note, and the fret distance, measured from the first note (C).

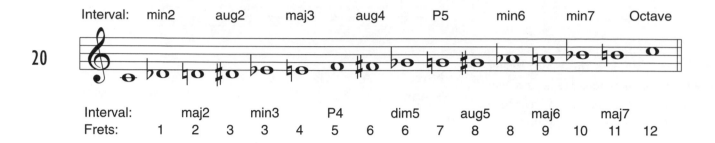

Interval:		maj2		min3		P4		dim5		aug5		maj6		maj7	
Frets:	1	2	3	3	4	5	6	6	7	8	8	9	10	11	12

Here is a table of interval abbreviations.

min2 = minor 2nd	P4 = perfect 4th	min6 = minor 6th
maj2 = major 2nd	aug4 = augmented 4th	maj6 = major 6th
aug2 = augmented 2nd	dim5 = diminished 5th	min7 = minor 7th
min3 = minor 3rd	P5 = perfect 5th	maj7 = major 7th
maj3 = major 3rd	aug5 = augmented 5th	

You may have noticed that some intervals, such as the dim5 (G♭) and the aug4 (F♯) have the same fret distance. When two different notes are played on the same fret and have the same pitch, they are said to be *enharmonically equivalent*.

THE NUMBERING SYSTEM

To facilitate musical discussion and understanding between musicians, we use a system of numbering which is directly related to the major scale. The notes of a major scale are numbered as follows:

Key of C Major

1	2	3	4	5	6	7
C	D	E	F	G	A	B

All other chord and scale spellings relate to this system.

INTERVAL INVERSION

To *invert* an interval is to turn it upside down—raising the lower note one octave or by lowering the top note one octave.

Also, the *quality* of the chord (whether it is major, minor or perfect) will change to its opposite, except for perfect intervals. They will remain perfect. For example:

Major becomes **Minor**
Minor becomes **Major**
Perfect remains **Perfect**

We use the major scale built on the bottom note of an interval as a measuring device. In the next example, the distance between G and E in the G Major scale is that of a major 6th. Inverting and using the E Major scale to measure the new interval, we find the interval is now a minor 3rd. In the second example using the A Major scale, we find the distance between an A and a C to be a minor third. After inversion, using the C Major scale to measure up from the bottom note will reveal the new interval to be a major 6th.

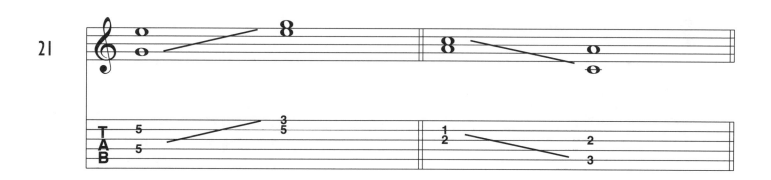

21

An easy way to figure out interval inversions is to realize that the sum of both intervals — the original interval and the inverted interval—will always equal nine. An inverted 2nd will become a 7th (2+7=9), and an inverted 3rd will become a 6th (3+6=9), etc.

$$+ \quad \frac{\begin{matrix} 1 \\ 8 \end{matrix}}{9} \quad \frac{\begin{matrix} 2 \\ 7 \end{matrix}}{9} \quad \frac{\begin{matrix} 3 \\ 6 \end{matrix}}{9} \quad \frac{\begin{matrix} 4 \\ 5 \end{matrix}}{9} \quad \frac{\begin{matrix} 5 \\ 4 \end{matrix}}{9} \quad \frac{\begin{matrix} 6 \\ 3 \end{matrix}}{9} \quad \frac{\begin{matrix} 7 \\ 2 \end{matrix}}{9} \quad \frac{\begin{matrix} 8 \\ 1 \end{matrix}}{9}$$

If you found this section difficult to follow, come back to it after you are very familiar with the major scale in all the keys.

CHORDS

Knowing about *chords* is absolutely necessary for playing the blues. But, thankfully, it's easy! Two or more notes played together is called a chord. Usually, a chord will have three or more notes. A three note chord is called a *triad*. As in major scale construction, a chord is always built up from a root. The intervallic relationships of the notes in the chord to the root determines the chord type. There are four basic triad types: *major*, *minor*, *augmented* and *diminished*.

MAJOR

Major chords always use the root (1), 3rd (3), and 5th (5) notes of the major scale.

D Major:	1	3	5
	D	F♯	A

Play a D major chord on your guitar. Notice that the best sounding, most convenient way to play chords on the guitar almost always involves reorganizing the notes, and even doubling (or tripling!) some of them. This is called *voicing*. It's OK! As long as a chord has the root, 3rd and 5th, it's a major chord. They need not appear in order in your fingering. See, I told the truth, it's really easy!

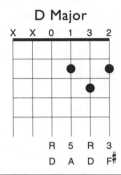

D Major

MINOR

Minor chords use the root (1), minor 3rd (♭3), and 5th (5) notes taken from the root of the chord. A ♭3 refers to lowering the third note of the major scale by one half step. Get the idea? GOOD!

D Minor:	1	♭3	5
	D	F	A

DIMINISHED

Diminished chords use the root (1), minor 3rd (♭3) and flat 5th (♭5).

D Diminished:	1	♭3	♭5
	D	F	A♭

AUGMENTED

Augmented chords use the root (1), 3rd (3) and sharp 5th (♯5).

D Augmented:	1	3	♯5
	D	F♯	A♯

SEVENTH CHORDS

Here are four kinds of 7th chords. The dominant 7th (7) is the most common. Minor 7th chords (min7) and diminished 7th (dim7) are also used. The major 7th (Maj7) type is rarely used in the blues.

D7	1	3	5	♭7
	D	F♯	A	C
Dmin7	1	♭3	5	7
	D	F	A	C
Ddim7	1	♭3	♭5	♭♭7
	D	F	A♭	C♭
D Maj7	1	3	5	7
	D	F♯	A	C♯

CHORD EXTENSIONS

In your travels you may have encountered strange and wondrous numbers attached to chords like 9, 11, 13, etc. These are chord extensions. They refer to chords that have at least four notes. Remember the major scale? The eighth note is the same as the first. What do you think nine is the same as? You guessed it—2 is the same as 9, only 9 is an octave higher. So this is how these numbers relate to the major scale.

1	2	3	4	5	6	7
	(9)		(11)		(13)	

9 is the same as **2** only an octave higher.
11 is the same as **4** only an octave higher.
13 is the same as **6** only an octave higher.

DOMINANT CHORDS

Dominant chords, chords with a ♭7, are the stock and trade chords for the blues. Blues players never leave home without them. (Dominant chords can be easily identified because they could be bingo-calls: G7, C9, A13, BINGO!!).

Here are the dominant chord formulas, using the numbering system in D Major.

D Dominant 7th (D7)	1	3	5	♭7		
	D	F♯	A	C		

D Dominant 9th (D9)	1	3	5	♭7	9	
	D	F♯	A	C	E	

11th chords are less commonly used in blues (they have a very jazzy sound). Here is the formula:

Dominant 11th (D11)	1	3	5	♭7	11	
	D	F♯	A	C	G	

Dominant 13th (D13)	1	3	5	♭7	9	13
	D	F♯	A	C	E	B

Using these formulas will allow you to play the blues and figure out the notes in the chords in any key. Here is a quick worksheet. Write out the scales and refer to them as guides for building the chords.

What are the notes in the following chords? If you want, you can write out the major scales for each chord, then apply the formulas for each specific chord. Here is an example of how to do this exercise:

C7	1	3	5	$\flat 7$
	C	E	G	$B\flat$

Fill in the notes for the following chords. Turn the book upside down for the answers.

A7	1	3	5	$\flat 7$		
	__	__	__	__		

D9	1	3	5	$\flat 7$	9	
	__	__	__	__	__	

Edim	1	$\flat 3$	$\flat 5$
	__	__	__

GAug	1	3	$\sharp 5$
	__	__	__

FMaj	1	3	5
	__	__	__

B13	1	3	5	$\flat 7$	9	13
	__	__	__	__	__	__

CHORD SCALES—DIATONIC HARMONY

Diatonic is a fancy sounding word—not bluesy at all—but its definition is simple. It means "within the key." So, if you are playing only notes or chords that come from one major scale, you are playing *diatonically*. (Not to be confused with diabolically, which is something altogether different.)

The chord scale is what happens when you build a triad on every note of a major scale. These are the diatonic chords, and they are categorized by Roman numerals so they can be used in any key. The upper case Roman numerals indicate a major chord. Lower case Roman numerals are used for minor triads, and lower case Roman numerals with a "°" indicates a diminished triad. All three of these basic chord types occur in a major key. As you know, the quality of the major and minor chords is defined by the 3rd of the chord, and the diminished chord gets its sound from a ♭3 and ♭5.

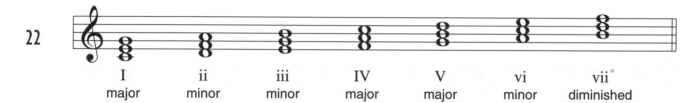

22

I	ii	iii	IV	V	vi	vii°
major	minor	minor	major	major	minor	diminished

Here is a chord scale with 7th chords. Notice that only the V chord becomes a dominant type chord (the 7th is a

I7	ii7	iii7	IV7	V7	vi7	vii°7
Maj7	min7	min7	Maj7	Dom7	min7	1/2dim7

minor 7th, or ♭7, above the root of the chord). The diminished chord becomes a *half-diminished 7th* chord (shown as °, it's built, 1, ♭3, 5, ♭7).

Here is where the blues "breaks the rules." We use dominant 7th chords all over the place! Typically, we will play dominant 7th chords on I, IV and V.

CHORD SCALE QUIZ

What are the I7, IV7 and V7 chords for the following keys?

Example: Key of C: C7   F7   G7

All of them are dominant type 7th chords. Turn the book upside down for the correct answers

	I	IV	V
Key of D	___	___	___
Key of A	___	___	___
Key of G	___	___	___
Key of E	___	___	___
Key of B♭	___	___	___

Correct answers:

D = D7, G7, A7
A = A7, D7, E7
G = G7, C7, D7
E = E7, A7, B7
B♭ = B♭7, E♭7, F7

THE TWELVE-BAR BLUES

MAJOR BLUES

A *twelve-bar blues* is a twelve measure *chord progression* (series of related chords) using the I, IV and V chords of a particular key. In the key of D Major, for instance, I is D, IV is G and V is A. A Major blues typically uses dominant chords. For that reason we often refer to a major blues as a dominant blues. The important thing here is that a twelve-bar blues progression will almost always proceed the same way. Here is how the I7, IV7 and V7 chords will come together (the slashes represent the four beats of each measure):

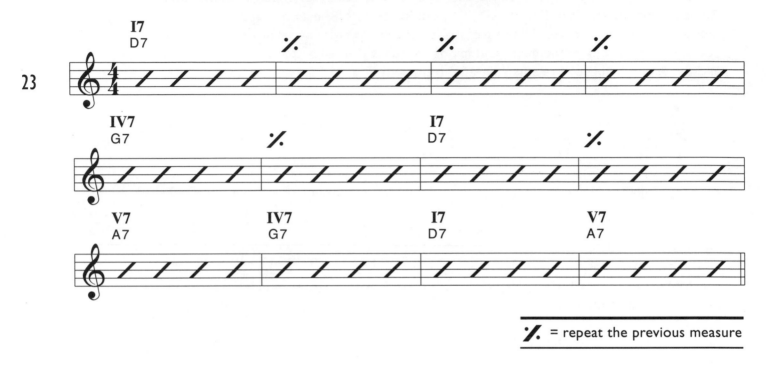

% = repeat the previous measure

MINOR BLUES

In a minor blues, we are still dealing with a I-IV-V progression, but the chords are now minor 7ths (min7) instead of dominant sevenths. Here is a standard twelve-bar minor blues in A Minor.

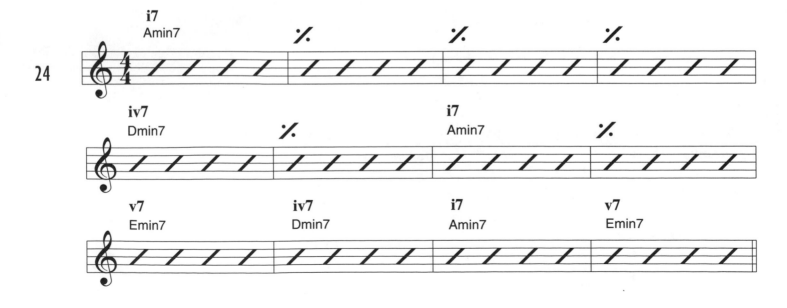

CHAPTER 3

Blues Rhythm Guitar

SWING EIGHTHS

WOW! We have a lot to talk about here! Let's start with the concept of *swing eighths and straight eighths*. Straight eighth notes are counted evenly—"one-+-two-+-three-+-four-+." Swing eighths are counted with a whole different feel. Technically, swing eighths have a *triplet* feel. Triplets are what happens when one beat is divided into three equal parts (see page 11). Sometimes, swing eighths are written just like straight eighths and it assumed that the expert player will know to swing it. Sometimes they are written as dotted-eighth/sixteenth note combinations, and sometimes they are written as quarter/eighth triplet combinations, as in the second measure of the example below.

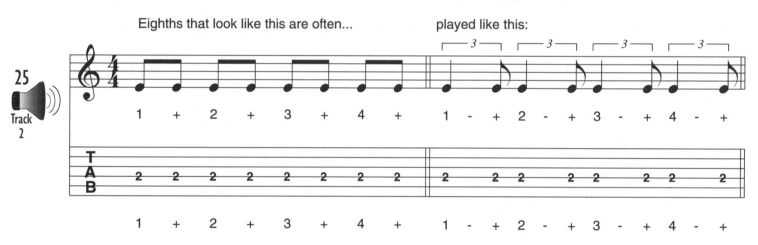

A good analogy for swing eights would be the clopping horse hoofs in the song "Happy Trails." Remember the bum—ba-<u>dee</u>—da-bum—ba-<u>dee</u>—da-bum, etc? Now count "one— + two—+ three—+ four—+ one," etc. When musicians talk about playing a shuffle they are speaking of this swing eighth feel. A straight eighth feel would be the groove of "Johnny B. Goode" by Chuck Berry while the swing eighth feel, or shuffle, would be the groove in "Little Sister" by Stevie Ray Vaughan. Think about some of your favorite blues tunes and which of them are shuffles ("Sweet Home Chicago," "Dust My Broom," "Statesboro Blues") and which are straight eighths ("Born Under a Bad Sign, " "The Thrill Is Gone," "Crossroads").

BOOGIE!

In this section of the book, we are going to look at many styles of rhythms. The following exercises are "boogie" rhythms, typified by using the lower strings in twos and threes to create a hefty low end chunk.

Here is a boogie pattern based on the low E string with some bass movement. Try it in straight and swing feels.

The same rhythm, but moved up the neck to the key of G. Again, try it in both feels. Closed position patterns like this lend themselves to *left hand muting*. Right after plucking the first eight note of each beat, lift your left hand fingers off the frets, but leave them on the strings. This will cause the note to sound shortened, or *staccato*.

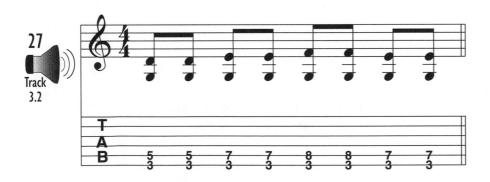

The bass movement is slightly more complex in this example.

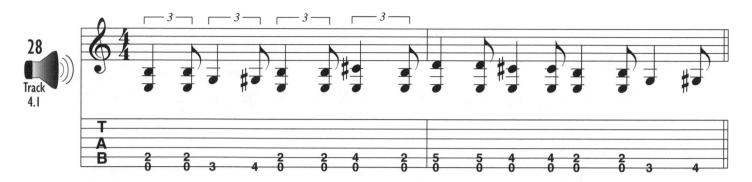

This is a similar rhythm, but with more movement in the upper voice. Try swinging the eigthths.

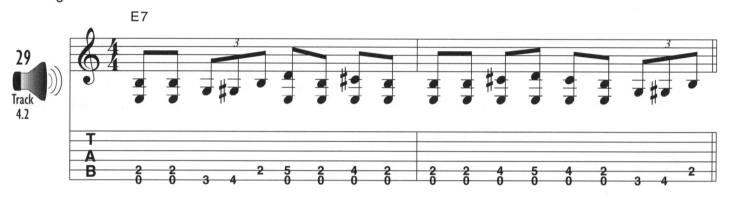

This example is a typical Muddy Waters "I'm a Man" riff in A.

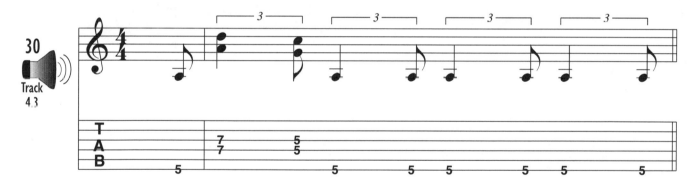

This is a strumming rhythm/boogie riff using a bass note on the downbeats with the open first and second strings on the upbeats a la Stevie Ray Vaughn.

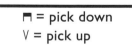

⊓ = pick down
V = pick up

Here is a full twelve-bar boogie using various boogie patterns. Notice that the triplet sign is only used in the first measure, although the rhythm continues throughout the example.

CHORD EXTENSIONS AND SUBSTITUTIONS

Now we begin our discussion of blues chords. Building a large knowledge of chords and knowing many ways to play each one, will definitely help you spice up your rhythm playing. First we will discuss the concept of *extensions*. I could go on at such great length about the theory of *chord substitution* that your eyes would become fuzzy and your brain would explode. Instead, I will refer you back to the theory chapter of this book, where extensions and substitutions are explained calmly and rationally.

The following chart is an expansion of the one on page 25, which showed the types of 7th chords found on each scale degree. This time, we also see the 9th, 11th and 13th chord types. Any of the extended chords in a column can be substituted for any of the other chords in that column.

I	ii	iii	IV	V	vi	vii	I
Major	minor	minor	Major	Major	minor	diminished	Major
Maj7	min7	min7	Maj7	Dom7	min7	dim7	Maj7
Maj9	min9	min9	Maj9	Dom9	min9	min7♭5	Maj9
Maj11	min11	min11	Maj11	Dom11	min11	min7♭5	Maj11
Maj6	min6	min6	Maj6	Dom13	min6	min7♭5	Maj6

Look at this chart as if you were choosing from a large menu at a family-style restaurant. You can choose one from column A, one from column B, etc. Suppose you are in the key of C Major. Instead of playing the same old boring C Major chord, you might choose to play a CMaj7, or a CMaj9, whichever was the sound you were looking for. You could use any chord in that column. The same holds true for any chord in the key. You can mix and match and trade them with your friends.

Magic Sam

DOMINANT BLUES SUBSTITUTIONS

On page 25 of Chapter 2 you learned how a major blues primarily uses dominant chords on I, IV and V (remember the bingo-call analogy from page 23?). So, in an A Major blues, the I chord is A7, the IV chord is D7 and the V chord is E7. With chord extension substitution you may substitute any dominant chord. Your choices are shown on the right:

I	IV	V
A7	D7	E7
A9	D9	E9
A11*	D11*	E11*
A13	D13	E13

These jazzy chords don't sound much like the blues.

All of this may mean nothing to you without chord forms to work with, so retire to your favorite practice space and work on these!

DOMINANT CHORD FORMS

A few different voicings are shown for each chord. Notice where the roots are located.

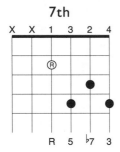

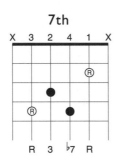

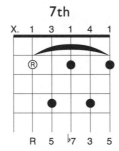

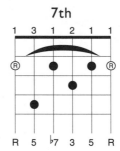

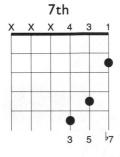

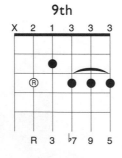

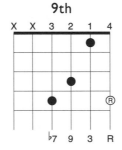

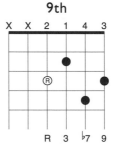

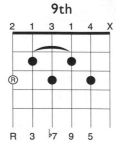

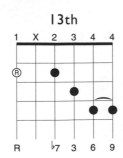

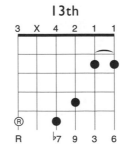

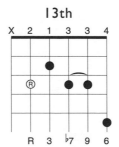

Here are some twelve-bar blues progressions using these chord forms in three keys: E, A, and B♭.

33

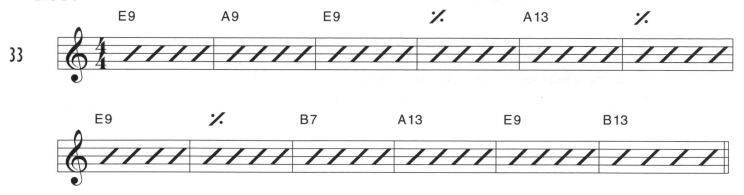

34

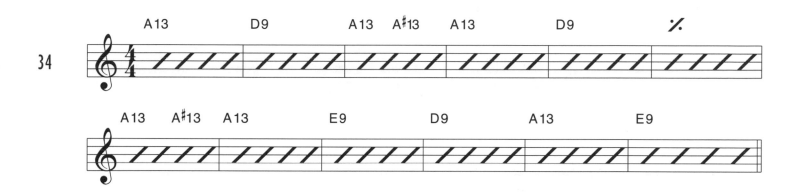

35

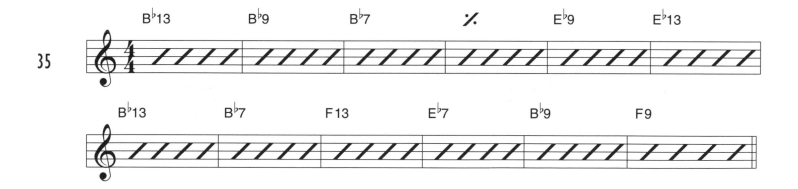

Like dominant blues chords, minor blues chords can be substituted. There is nothing like a slow minor blues to tear your heart out! Again, the more chord forms you know, the more exciting and moving the song. We will go deeper into minor and dominant blues forms later in the book. Now, back to your practice room and learn these chord forms.

MINOR CHORD FORMS

As with the dominant chords, keep track of where the root is located.

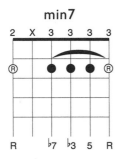

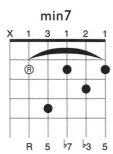

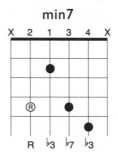

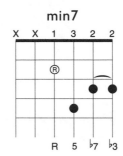

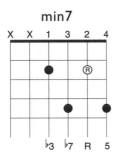

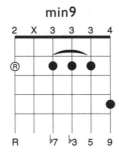

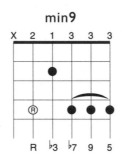

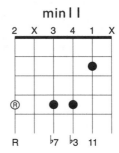

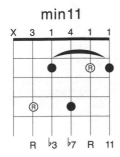

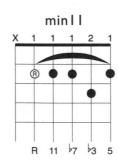

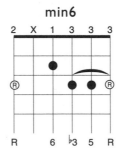

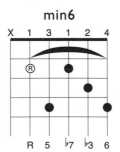

Here are some twelve-bar minor blues progressions using these chord forms in three keys: E Minor, A Minor and D Minor. Note the use of Dominant V chords.

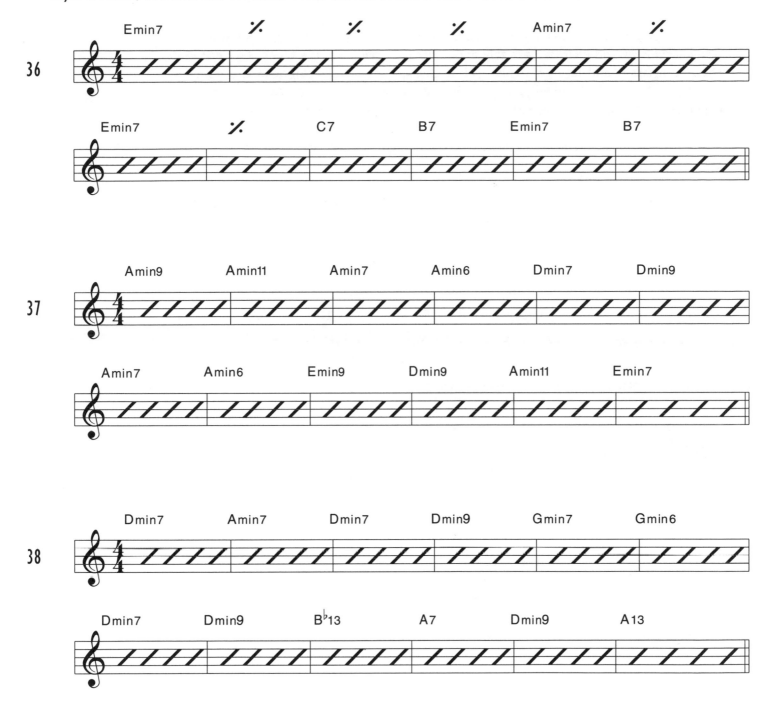

OK, now you have learned a lot of chord forms, but your rhythm playing might still sound bland, lackluster and lifeless. Let's talk about rhythm playing for the blues. Get out your cheap sunglasses and let's go! This, ⌐×, is a *chuck*. You'll be seeing it in the next few exercises. A "chuck" is when you strum *muted* strings. You *mute* by releasing left hand finger pressure from a chord, without removing your fingers from the strings.

There are two basic elements to good rhythm playing: 1) right and left hand interaction and 2) a steady tempo.

Let's start with one of the secrets of rhythm—the left hand. All the while, your right hand should be a machine, strumming relentlessly up and down. For shuffles use the swing eighth rhythm:

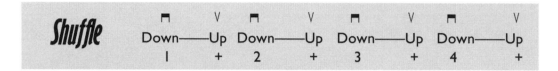

For funk or rock'n'roll rhythm use straight eighth strumming:

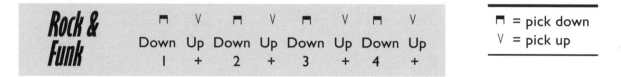

Here is a great rhythm technique to use for the following examples:

1) Keep the right hand strumming steady.
2) With the left hand, hold the chord.
3) Perform a chuck when you see this sign ⌐×.
4) Strum evenly up and down on your guitar. Count "one-and-two-and-three-and-four-and" as you strum in swing eighths.
5) Press down with your left hand when you see the regular chord slashes in the exercises.

This next example is the ever popular reggae rhythm.

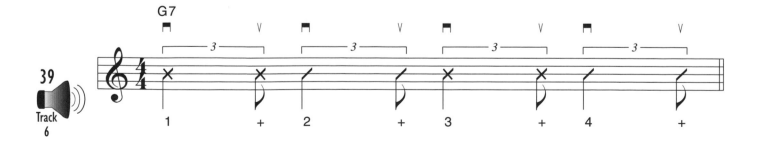

Comping is the art of laying down a simple, solid rhythm groove behind a singer or soloist. The following exercises explore accenting on the down stroke or up stroke of a strum using chord chucks.

Previously, we discussed the swing eighth note feel. Mute your strings with your left hand and get comfortable with the strumming pattern. Now finger the following A13 chord.

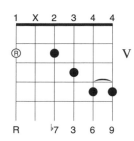

As you strum the shuffle pattern press your left hand down on the down stroke and mute on the upstroke.

Got it? Press down on 1, 2, 3 and 4, and release on the "ands."

Now let's finger a D9 chord.

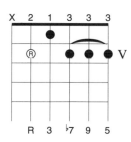

This time strum the shuffle rhythm and press down on the upstrokes and release the pressure on the downstrokes.

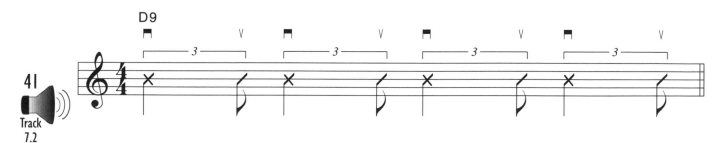

Pretty cool, isn't it? Now let's combine both patterns on a two measure vamp.

Now here's a twelve-bar blues in A using this method.

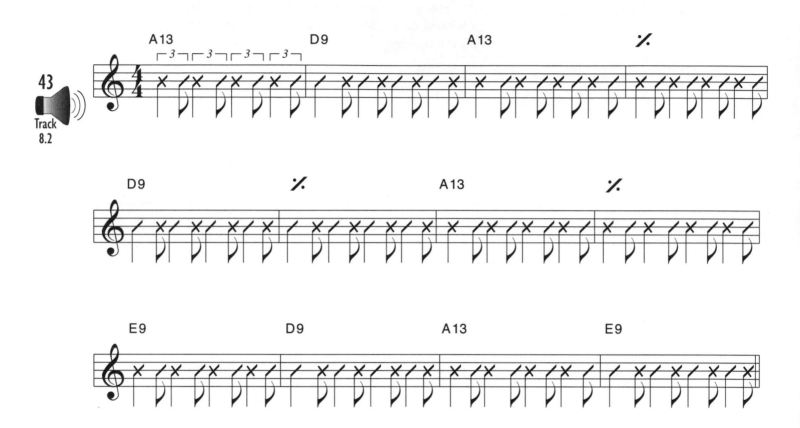

This is just an example. There is no particular reason why I chose to accent down strokes with a chuck on the I chord and up strokes on the IV chord other than it sounds good. You may accent either way on any chord. Accenting with chucks sure spices up your rhythm, doesn't it?

SLIDING CHORD FORMS

In a slide, the left hand moves quickly up or down to the next note or chord, which is usually not picked with the right hand. This expressive effect is marked with the sign ╱, an "S" in the TAB and, if it is to happen quickly, small *grace notes* (♪) in the standard music notation (for instance, see Example 44, page 40).

There is an interesting relationship between 6th chords and 9th chords. Both have a pretty, melodic sound and they are very similar in fingering, especially on the upper strings.

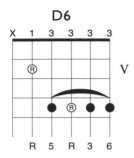

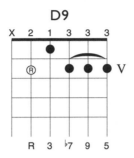

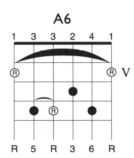

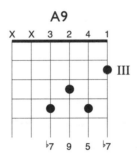

See the similarity in fingering on the upper strings?   Because of their similarities, and because they both lend themselves to easy movement around the neck of the guitar, these chords are often used together in rhythm parts that involve slides. You have probably heard this countless times on blues albums. A good example is the Allman Brother's version of "Stormy Monday" on the *Fillmore East* album, or Stevie Ray Vaughan's "Empty Arms" on *The Sky is Crying* album.

Here is a twelve-bar blues rhythm using sliding chord forms in the key of A Major. Swing the eighths.

FUNKY BLUES RHYTHM FILLS

BORROWING TRIADS FROM ANOTHER KEY

A *fill* is a line or group of chords used to add interest and motion to a rhythm part. Fills occur between the primary chords of a progression, which is why we call them fills. Some cool funky fills can be created by using the chords from the key of the current chord in the progression, rather than from the key of the progression. Since dominant chords are considered V of a major key, you can use the major key in which that dominant chord is diatonic (see Chapter 2, page 25) to create fills for the chord.

Suppose you are jamming on a stationary E9 chord, groovin' away in a blues in E. You can spice up that funky rhythm some harmonic color. Here's how it's done.

Since E9 is considered a dominant chord and dominant chords are considered V chords of a major key, you need only deduce which key it is that has E as the V. You can then use the chords of that major key, in this case, A Major, to spice up your rhythm with some fills. Here is a quick and easy way to find out the key from which a dominant chord is derived. We will use E9 as an example.

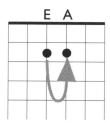

Find the note E on your second, fourth, fifth or sixth string. For example, there is an E on the second fret, fourth string. To find what key uses E as the V chord, simply play the note directly across from the E on the next highest string, same fret. This note, (A), would be found on the second fret, third string.

You may play partial chords or triads in the key of A Major to embellish your rhythms when you would otherwise be stumin' away on your E9, even though you're playing a blues in E. Notice that this technique does not work if you start from a note on the third string, because of the guitar's tuning. The interval from the third to second string is different (a 3rd instead of a 4th), so this method would find the wrong key. In this case go up a fret on the second string to find the right key.

The following basic chord forms work great for creating funky fills.

THREE BASIC TRIAD FORMS

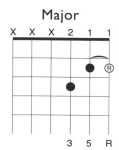
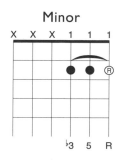
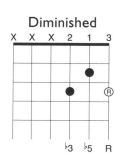

Since you are groovin' on an E9 chord, the V chord in A Major, familiarize yourself with the chords from A Major.

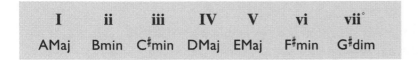

I	ii	iii	IV	V	vi	vii°
AMaj	Bmin	C#min	DMaj	EMaj	F#min	G#dim

Now you know what chords to use to create fills for an E9 chord. Let's hear how they sound in context.

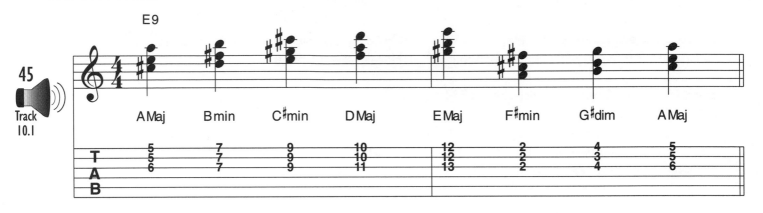

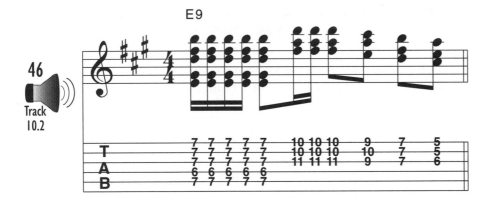

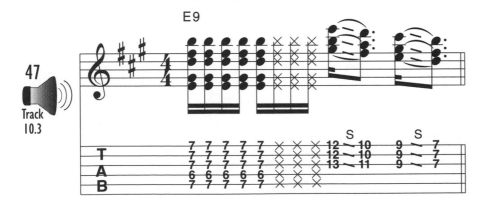

The next example is a funky twelve-bar blues in E with chord fills. When on the I chord (E9) the fills are in A Major. When on the IV chord (A13) the fills are in D Major. When on the V chord (B13) the fills are in E Major. This is a rhythm concept well worth taking some time with! It's kind of tough at first because you really have to think fast, but with practice it will become second nature.

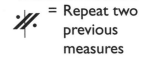
= Repeat two previous measures

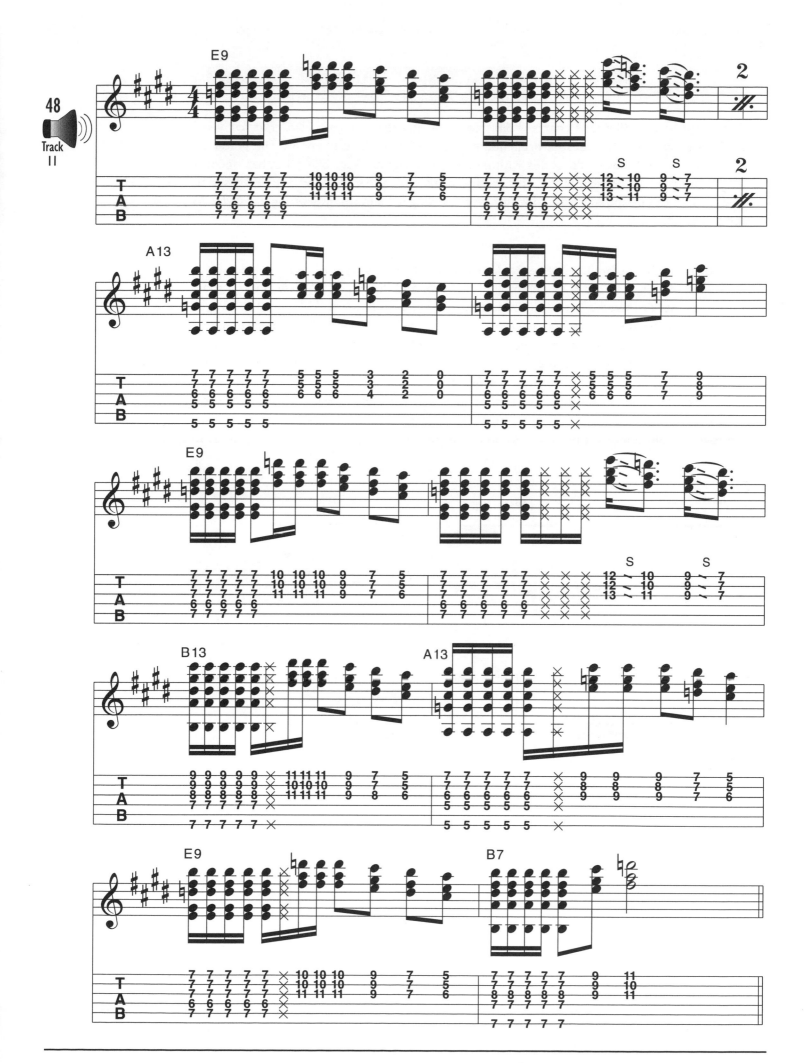

RHYTHM & BLUES FILLS

According to the Billboard charts "R&B" now means urban dance music. But for years R&B meant the good-time, soul-drenched music of Motown and Memphis. The guitarists of this era fused blues guitar styles with a funky, street-smart sensibility that has become an integral part of modern blues. This section deals with a few of the various R&B styles. These ideas can be integrated into your rhythm styling for a more interesting bag of tricks for the blues.

Let's begin with the familiar Stevie Ray Vaughan/Jimi Hendrix style of chordal fills. Great examples of this are "Little Wing" by Jimi Hendrix and "Lenny" by Stevie Ray Vaughan. Obviously, Stevie owed a lot of his styling to Jimi's previous work. What is not so well known was Jimi's debt to the influence of Curtis "Superfly" Mayfield, who wrote such R&B standards as "People Get Ready." The basic premise of this concept is to seamlessly weave fills around a chord. There are several well used major and minor chord forms that are integral to this style. This is because the fills are created primarily by hammering-on to, and pulling-off from, other scale tones that surround the chords, and these chord forms lend themselves to that kind of treatment. These are open chord forms that have been made moveable, and are therefore usable in any key.

G Major Type
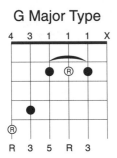

C Major Type
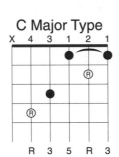

F Major Type
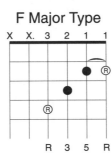

E Minor 7 Type
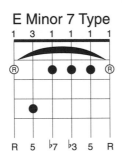

A Minor 7 Type
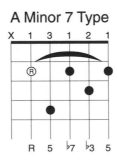

Let's begin with an example using the G Major type form as a C chord. The G Major type form becomes a C chord simply by moving the chord so that the sixth string root is on the eighth fret (C). Hammer-ons and pull-offs create the fills.

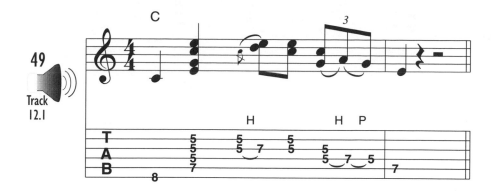

Now here is one using a C major type chord form as an F Major. Again, just play the C Major type form with an F root.

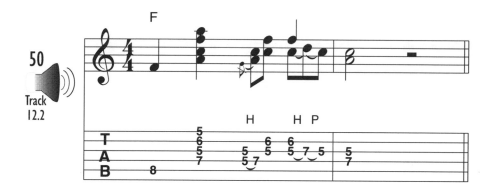

Now let's examine a fill using an F Major type chord form as a C Major.

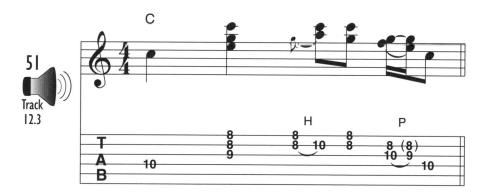

Notice that a new kind of grace note is introduced in Example 49.

For our purposes, the slash indicates that this note is played right on the beat, at the same time as the note above it. Since it's only a grace note, the hammer-on to the next note is executed immediately.

This example uses the previous three chord forms in a cool R&B I-IV progression.

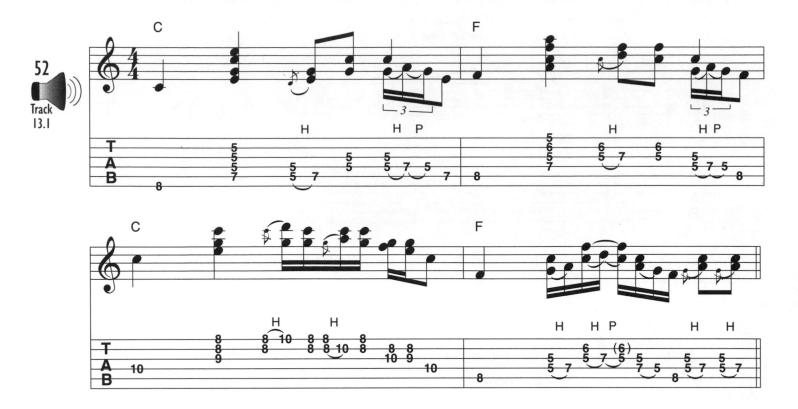

Here is an example using the E Minor 7 type chord form as an Amin7.

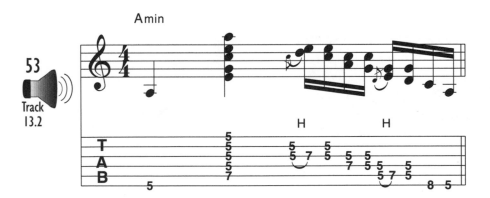

This example uses the A Minor 7 type chord form as a Dmin7.

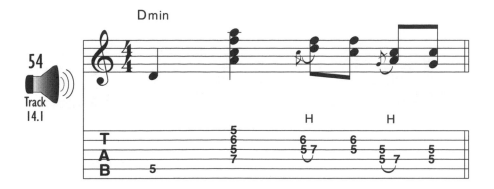

Here is an example using a minor i-iv progression, Amin7 to Dmin7.

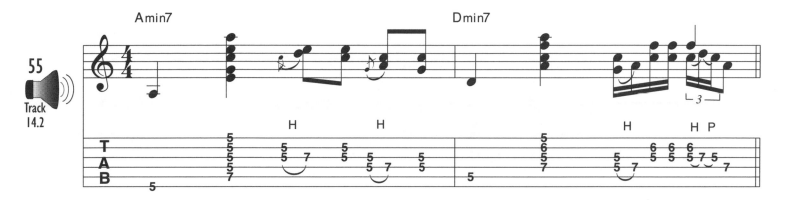

Jimi Hendrix

Let's combine all of these forms by using them to embellish a I-vi-ii-V progression in C Major (C, Amin7, Dmin7, G).

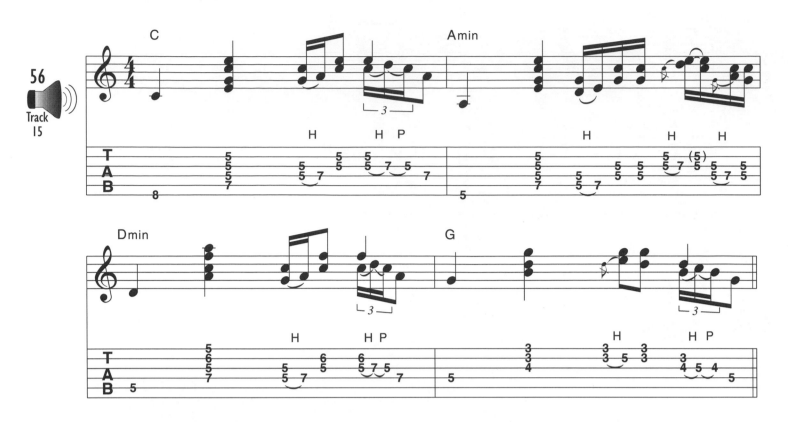

Eric Clapton

When you combine these concepts with those learned in the Funky Blues Rhythm section, you will be on your way to being a great rhythm player! Here's an example on a stationary E9 chord using all of this stuff together.

Stevie Ray Vaughn

SECRETS OF THE BLUES!

Blues Philosophy

Since this is an intermediate book, it is safe to assume that you have been playing for a while. Before we get into the soloing section of this book we should have a little talk. Blues guitar is not just a style, but a life-style and a philosophy. There is a school of thought that says one cannot learn blues guitar from a book. While this is untrue, it is true that the emotional side of playing comes from within, rather than from a book or teacher. To learn the blues one must have the ability to tap into your soul and make it come pouring out through your instrument. You can't get "soul" from a book or any other person. It has to come from deep within yourself. This involves a great deal of soul searching and being comfortable with dragging out the pain and insecurities in your life. You can only play what you have lived. This definitely does **not** mean you have to suffer, drink whisky, or be born the son or daughter of a poor sharecropper! It means you have to dig at the well of your most deeply buried emotions. I know, now you're thinking "What is this? The zen of blues guitar?" Maybe it is! When you are truly one with your instrument, when you can actualize any melody that comes into your mind, that is the greatest feeling in the world. It will keep you sane.

A lot of my students come to me and say "I'm playing all the same notes as B. B. but it doesn't sound like him!" Of course it doesn't sound like B. B. You aren't B. B. You are a unique individual with your own hopes and dreams. You should try and sound like *you*.

Here is an exercise designed to bring your emotions to the surface. Take a sheet of paper and a pen and find a quiet spot where you won't be bothered. Write down how you really feel about yourself, your life, your family, your career and your loved ones. You don't even need to use complete sentences. *Let it all out!* All of the things that you've never told anyone. Be completely and utterly honest with yourself. When you're done, read it back. It is very hard to face your own personal demons but that is your life. Now play a slow minor blues like you have never played it before. Do you feel it? When you really play the blues there is an electric feeling that courses through your body. If you've never felt that feeling, don't worry. You will know it when it comes. That is what great guitarists tap into when they play.

As you continue into the soloing section of this book, keep in mind that music is an art and art is a deeply personal thing. It's OK to be different than everyone else. It's great to have your own style. Strive to touch greatness. This is the fundamental difference between somebody who plays guitar and an **artist**.

Whew! Had enough? Now we can resume our regularly scheduled program.

CHAPTER 4

A Quick Technique Review

The two most expressive tools a blues guitarist has are vibrato and string bending. In this chapter we will explore both of these essential techniques. This is an important prelude to our study of blues lead guitar.

BENDING

One of the most important blues guitar techniques is, of course, bending. Bending accuracy is what separates mature players from beginners. The following examples will help you develop accuracy by comparing your bent notes to unbent notes. Listen and make sure you're bending to the right pitch! Notice the use of the small grace notes to indicate the note on which the bend begins. These notes are very quick. Pluck and then bend right away!

HALF STEP BENDS

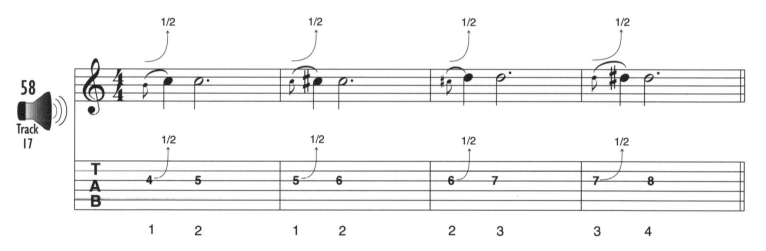

WHOLE STEP BENDS

REVERSE BENDING

This is an important one. Bend quickly up to the notes, and then bend back down more slowly, in rhythm, without plucking again.

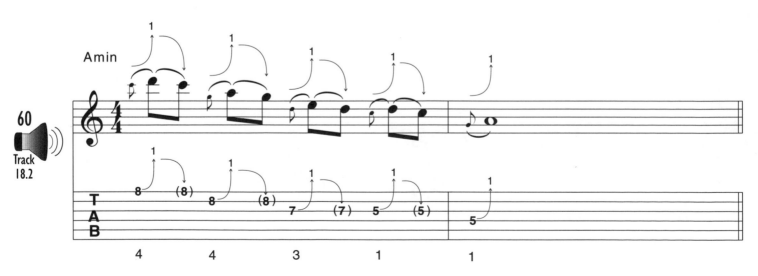

VIBRATO

You may have heard some version of the story of B. B. King absolutely leveling a pair of English blues guitarists (Clapton, Page) in a playing contest with a single note! Why is it that some guitarists have an instantly identifiable sound? A lot has to do with their tone but another major factor is their signature vibrato. When playing blues, the thicker, more intense the player's vibrato is, the better.

Vibrato is a very quick bend and release. It is often indicated with this mark, or something like it: $\wedge\!\wedge\!\wedge$. The two kinds of vibrato we will be looking at are the standard resting note vibrato and the bent note vibrato. The kind that sends chills up your spine! *"BBBrrrrr."*

The biggest mistake most guitarists make when using vibrato is that they make it TOO THIN! Bend the string far enough to have a clear vibrato effect. Try to use a half step bend.

Practice bending in an eighth note rhythm. Pick only the first note.

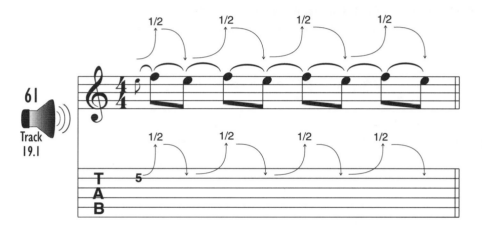

Now try it in sixteenth notes. Again, only the first note is picked.

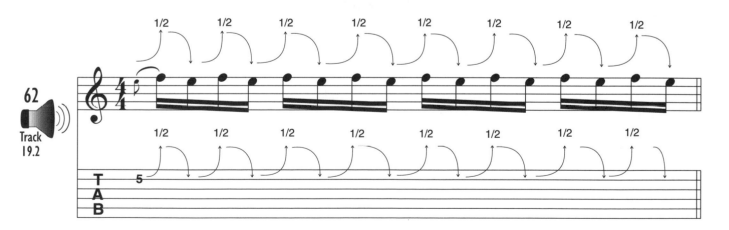

The other mistake most players make is pulling a note sharp. This is caused when you don't return to the natural resting point of the string each time you release the vibrato. Practice accurate vibrato by slowing down your vibrato and making sure when you release the bend you come back to the natural resting point of the string. This eliminates that "out of tune" sound.

A great way to test the effectiveness of your vibrato is to tape yourself. Listen for that sharp, consistent bend and release, not unlike an opera singer's vibrato. The tape doesn't lie. If you don't hear your vibrato on tape then you need to bend the string further. "If you ain't shakin' it, it ain't makin' it!" USE VIBRATO ANY TIME YOU PAUSE ON A NOTE! You simply can't use too much. It will make your playing sound much more mature and fluid.

BENT NOTE VIBRATO

Bent note vibrato is easily the most identifiable sound in blues guitar. Mastery of this effect will make you sound like you really know what you're doing on the "slab'o'wood with strings." This is the sound that scrunches up the faces of blues guitarists everywhere! *"Lord have mercy! Hallelujah!"* Oh! Sorry, I lost control for a second there! Anyway, this is how it should be done.

1) Bend up a whole step on the second string from G (eighth fret) to the sound of A (tenth fret).
2) Release the bend a half step, then re-bend up to A, release, bend, release, bend.
3) Repeat steps one and two, increasing the speed to eighth notes, then sixteenth notes.

EIGHTH NOTES. Only the first note is picked.

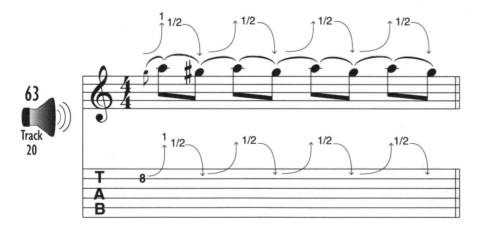

63 Track 20

SIXTEENTH NOTES

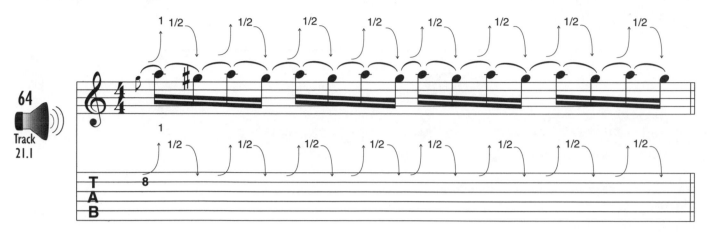

Another great expressive tool is to delay your vibrato until after you've bent a note.

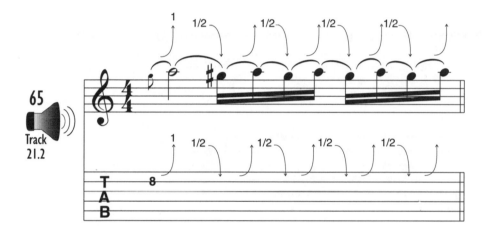

It is well worth your while to perfect these techniques. We will be using them throughout the rest of the book. A thorough knowledge of these techniques will make the licks on the following pages sound the way they should. So wha'd'ya waiting for? Back to your room and practice!

CHAPTER 5

Soloing

THE MINOR PENTATONIC SCALE

"Penta" is the Greek word for five and "tonics" means notes. By now most of you are familiar with the five note *minor pentatonic* wonder scale! For those of you who aren't, here is the formula, using the number system, and a full neck minor pentatonic scale in A Minor.

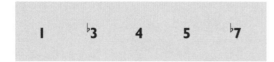

THE FIVE PATTERNS OF THE MINOR PENTATONIC SCALE

It's helpful to notice where each pattern begins on the sixth string. Also, learn the locations of the roots.

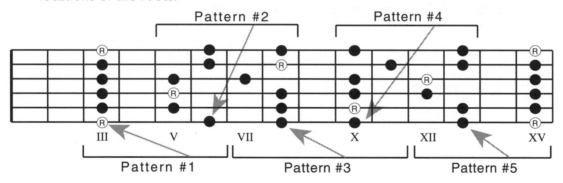

It's easy to find the minor pentatonic patterns in any key. You simply play Pattern #1 at the root of the key on the sixth string, and think five frets up to find where another pattern begins on the sixth string. Now patterns #3 and #5 will be easy to find, and #2 and #4 will follow. For example, in the key of G Major, the root is on the third fret, sixth string. So, you would play Pattern #1 starting on the third fret. Pattern #3 would start five frets up on the eighth fret. Eight plus five equals thirteen, so Pattern #5 would start on the thirteenth fret (or an octave lower on the first fret). Just remember: "penta" means five. Patterns #1, #3 and #5 are five frets apart. Pattern #2 starts on the second note of Pattern #1, and Pattern #4 starts on the second note of Pattern #3. Now calm down, wipe those beads of sweat off your forehead and remember guitar playing is FUN, FUN, FUN!

In the Key of G

Pattern	Fret	Formula	Next Fret
#1	III	III + 5	VIII
#3	VIII	VIII + 5	XIII or I
#5	XIII	2nd note of #1	VI
#2	VI	2nd note of #3	X
#4	X		

PHRASING

Before we get into the nuts and bolts of blues licks, we should talk about phrasing. Why do you think they call it phrasing? Great blues guitarists play in sentences, or "phrases." **The secret to playing great blues is to play like a blues singer sings.** Take a listen to some of your favorite blues players. First, listen to how they sing the verses. Then listen to the solo section. Do you hear the similarity in note placement? The guitarist will usually start and stop their phrases in the same spot as they would when singing the lyrics.

Try practicing this way:

Play along with one of your favorite blues singers. When they start singing, start playing. When they end their phrase, you end yours. So you are actually playing over the top of the vocalist. Be careful, if you do this when you are playing with a band, you may be out of a gig! This is to give you an idea of how to phrase your solos, not a way to do fills around a singer's lines.

Another great idea for phrasing is to hold your breath when you begin a phrase and release it when you end a phrase. This way, if you play too long without phrasing, you will turn blue and fall over. Phrasing seems preferable, don't you think?

Here are some other important ideas:

1) MOTIVIC DEVELOPMENT

If it sounds good, do it again! Don't be afraid to milk a good idea. Short distinctive, simple phrases, which lend themselves to repetition, are called *motives*. A motive will usually have very few notes. Not only can motives be repeated, but they can be moved around within the key.

Ronnie Earl

PHOTO • COURTESY OF RONNIE EARL

Here is an example of a three-note motive in A Minor Pentatonic. The motive is stated, then sequenced. A sequence is what it's called when a motive is repeated, starting on a different note each time.

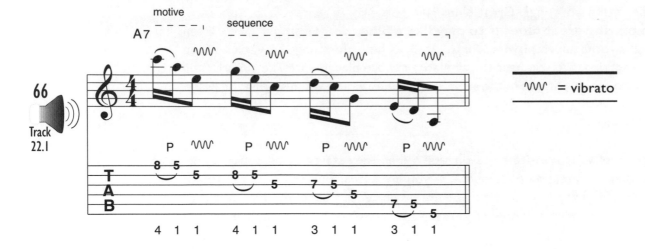

Here is a five-note motive, also in A Minor Pentatonic.

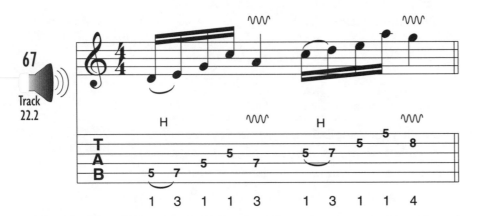

As you become more comfortable with this way of playing, you'll notice a big change in the way you solo. Your solos will seem more connected, more melodic. The people you jam with might even say "Hey, what happened to you? Been down to the crossroads?"

2) RHYTHMIC VARIATION

This aspect of guitar playing is extremely important for great solos. Try this: on a tape recorder, record a blues rhythm in A Major. As you listen back to your rhythm, try playing a solo using only one note (A on the first string, fifth fret). You can't bend it or slide up to it. You **can** use vibrato. You'll find the only way to play something interesting is to use dynamics (more on this next), and rhythmic variation. Try mixing up quarter, eighth, sixteenth notes, and eighth and sixteenth note triplets with varying dynamics. Use lots of quirky syncopation. Syncopation is when upbeats are stressed.

3) DYNAMICS

How soft or loud you attack your strings can be an incredibly expressive tool. A great guitarist can go from a whisper to a scream in the space of a few measures, drawing the listener into his solo. Again, the one note solo will make you very aware of this, as only dynamics and rhythmic variation will make it sound remotely interesting. Dynamics make your solos sound as if they are breathing. Certain notes will jump out from the rest when they are pinched harder than the others. Try this with your old familiar licks. Accent certain notes and play the others very softly. Move the accents around to different notes in the phrase. See how the whole lick is changed? Blues guitar is a study in dynamic contrast. Get this idea down, and you're well ahead of most guitarists!

Muddy Waters

Notice the use of rhythmic variation in the next two examples. Experiment with dynamics too!

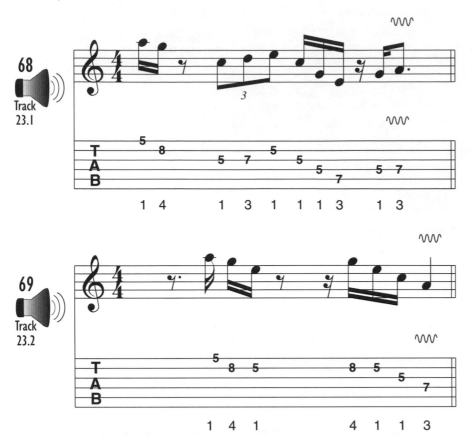

Albert Collins

NON-SCALE TONES

Non-scale tones are notes you hear blues guitarists use that aren't in the minor pentatonic scale. They add a distinctive flavor and finesse to your solos. They are sometimes called *passing tones* because you often pass through them on your way to another note in the scale. Not all non-scale tones, however, are strictly passing tones. There are many ways to approach and leave non-scale tones. Just don't end phrases on them or you will be out of key.

The non-scale tones we will be incorporating into the minor pentatonic scale are the ♭2, 2, ♭5, 6 and 7 tones of the major scale of the root of the key. These are the notes most often integrated into the solos of blues and blues/rock guitarists. Let's start by incorporating these notes into Pattern #1 of the minor pentatonic scale.

NON-SCALE TONES IN MINOR PENTATONIC PATTERN #1

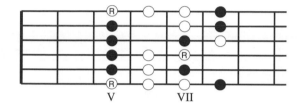

○ = passing tone

Here are some examples of licks in A Minor Pentatonic, using non-scale tones, bends, hammer-ons, pull-offs and vibrato! The passing tones are circled.

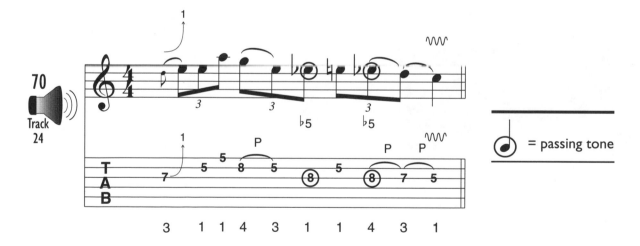

🎵 = passing tone

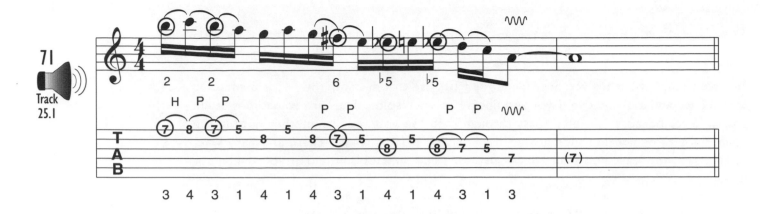

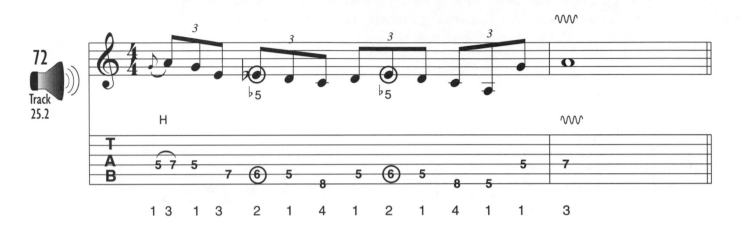

Buddy Guy

Albert King

Swing the eighths!

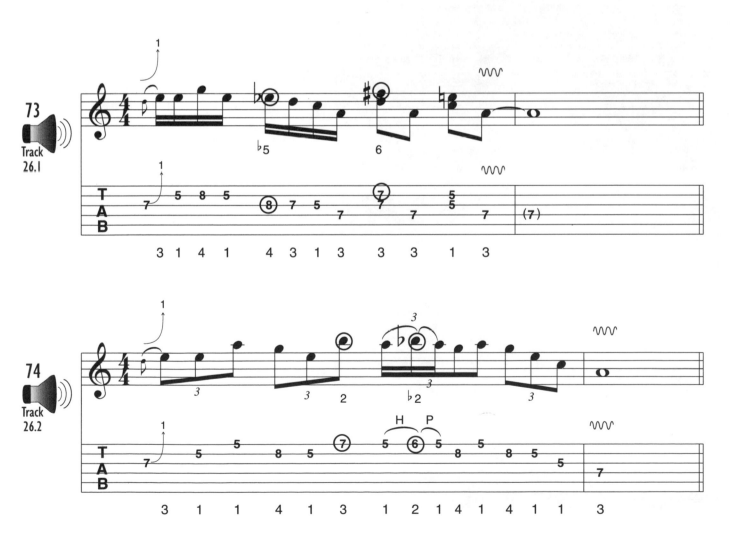

Here is how the non-scale tones are integrated into the remaining four patterns of the minor pentatonic scale.

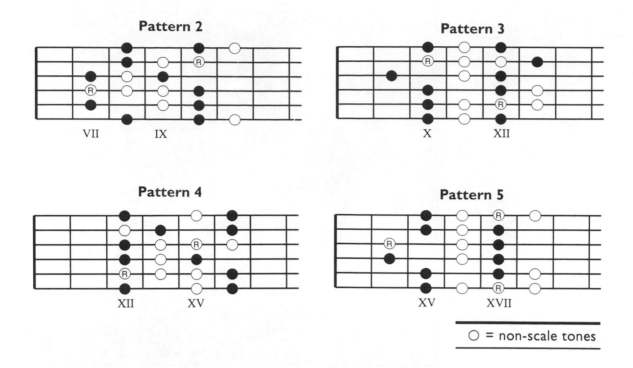

Pattern 2

VII   IX

Pattern 3

X   XII

Pattern 4

XII   XV

Pattern 5

XV   XVII

○ = non-scale tones

Freddie Green

Here are two common ways to break out of the box patterns. Both involve sliding a finger along a string from pattern to pattern. Note that there are two basic patterns in this form of movement. One with the root on the sixth string, and one with the root on the fifth string. Learn these and break out of the box! Amaze and impress your friends!

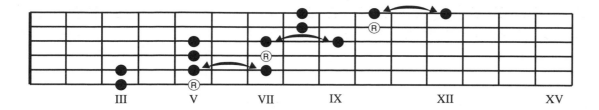

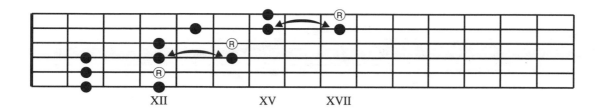

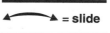 = slide

To do a slide, finger a note and pick it, then slide your left hand finger along the string, up or down the fretboard, to a new position. The notation for a slide in the music and TAB is just a diagonal line leading from the starting note up or down to the note you're meant to slide into, and an "S" in the TAB.

Here are some licks with non-scale tones, using different patterns of the minor pentatonic scale. Some of them demonstrate ways to combine different patterns. All of these licks are in A Minor.

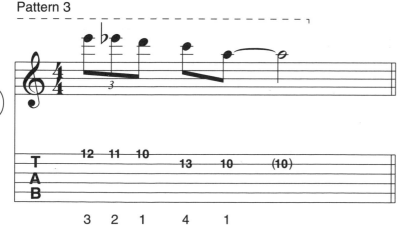

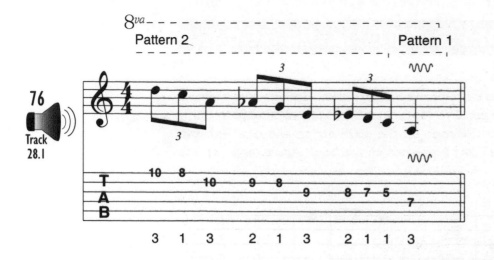

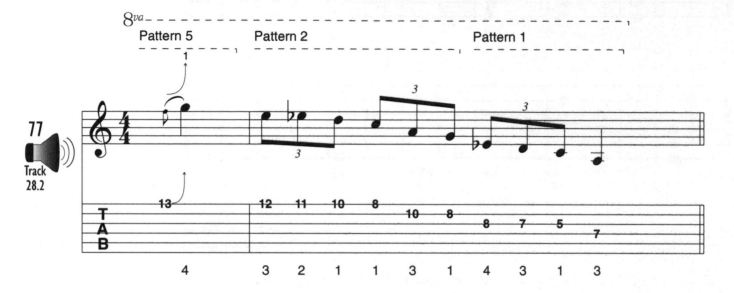

$8va$ = Play an octave higher than written.

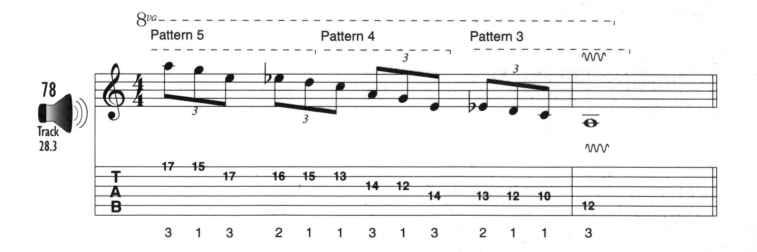

Here is the formula for the major pentatonic scale.

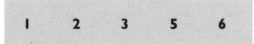

1	2	3	5	6

As the formula above indicates, a major pentatonic scale is the 1st, 2nd, 3rd, 5th and 6th notes of the major scale. An easy way to relate to major pentatonics is that in a major key, they are the exact same patterns as the minor pentatonics only three frets lower. So, if you are playing blues in A Major, you can move down three frets to F♯ and start the whole five pattern sequence from there. This is because F♯ is the relative minor key of A Major (see Chapter 2). Lots of you out there are aware of this, but for those of you who aren't, let's just illustrate this using Pattern #1:

For a Blues in A Major

A Minor Pentatonic

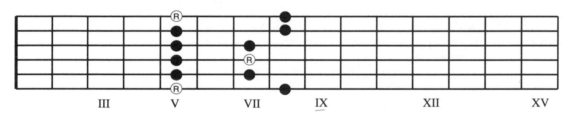

A Major Pentatonic

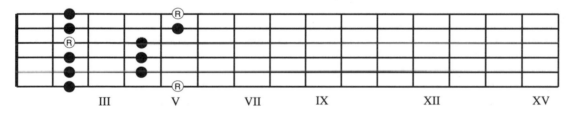

Here are some A Major Pentatonic, Pattern #1 licks. When playing major pentatonic, it is very important to resolve to the root of the key (in this case A). Notice the slide on the first note (see page 65).

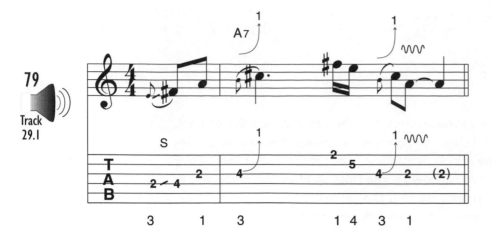

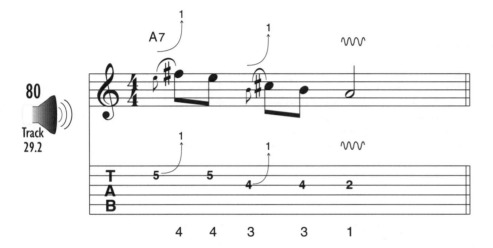

The next example lends itself to *shortpicking*. Move your thumb and index finger down to the edge of your pick and combine the skin of either finger with the pick as you strike the string. This produces a short or staccato note, sometimes producing bright *overtones* of other pitches as well.

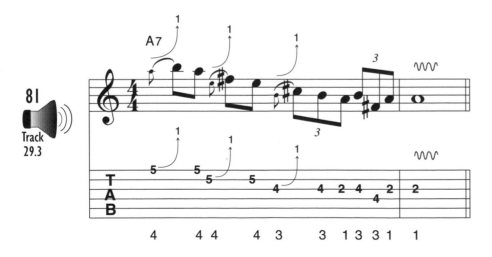

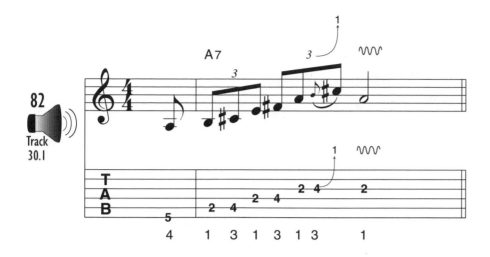

You may use any of the five patterns to play in A Major Pentatonic. Just use the F# Minor Pentatonic patterns, and as long as you resolve your licks to the root of the major key (A), you'll sound great. Here are some more licks in A Major Pentatonic using various patterns, all resolving to A.

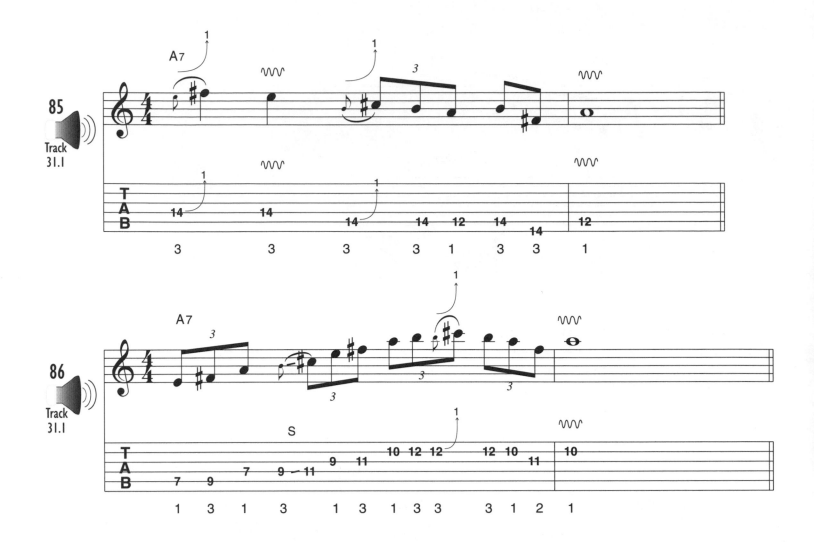

PHOTO • ROBERT KNOIGHT

Albert Lee

MIXING MAJOR AND MINOR PENTATONICS

One of the most identifiable sounds in blues is the integration of major pentatonic leads and fills with minor pentatonics in a major key. It is very important that you note **major pentatonics will not work in minor keys**. They only work in major keys.

Here is a general guideline:

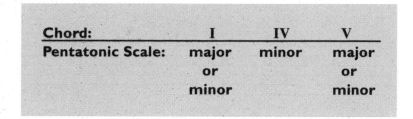

Chord:	I	IV	V
Pentatonic Scale:	major or minor	minor	major or minor

Over the I chord you may play either major or minor pentatonics. Over the IV chord you should stick to minor pentatonics. For the V chord, either major or minor pentatonics will do. Try these out with a major key blues.

Here is a diagram showing the overlapping of major and minor pentatonics in the key of A Major.

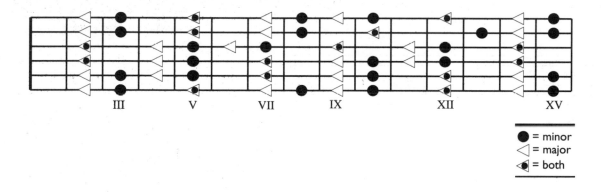

Here are some licks in the key of A Major which integrate minor and major pentatonics. The non-scale tones in the major pentatonic scale are the notes of the minor pentatonic scale. The minor pentatonic notes are circled.

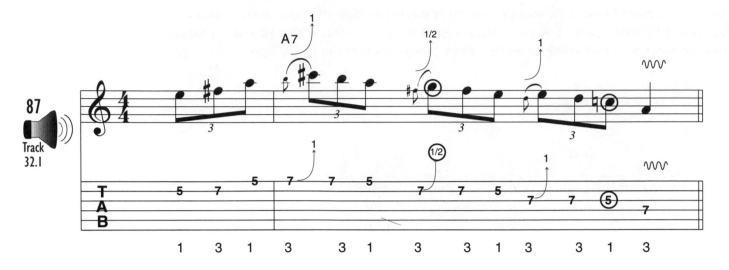

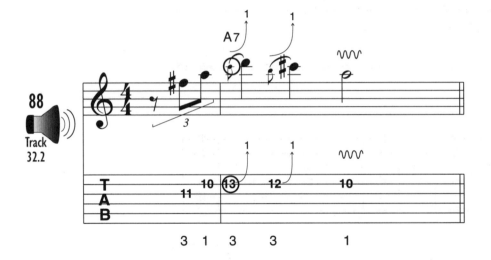

= Notes from the minor pentatonic scale. All others are from the major pentatonic scale.

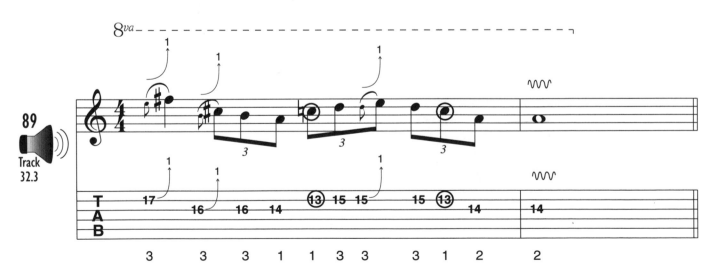

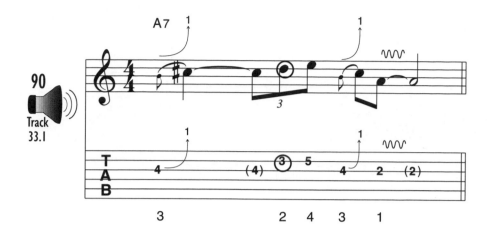

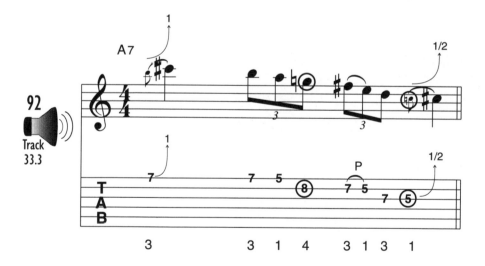

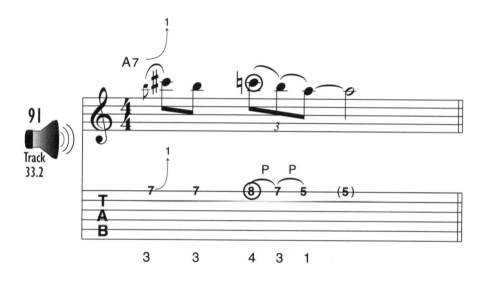

Things are starting to get a little interesting on the old guitar, aren't they? Well hold on to your seat—you ain't seen nothing yet.

CHAPTER 6

More About Soloing

RESOLVING TO 3 AND ♭7

Up to now, we have been resolving mostly on the root of the key. But the most colorful notes of dominant chords, which we use constantly, are the 3rd and the ♭7. Resolving to these notes will give a very melodic, bluesy sound to your solos. This is a sound used by many players, particularly the second generation English blues guitarists such as Eric Clapton, Jimmy Page and Gary Moore.

The relationship between ♭7 and 3 is a *tritone*. A tritone is an interval (distance) of three whole steps. This is the same as playing the root and the ♭5 of a key. Here is how it looks on the guitar:

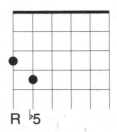

R ♭5

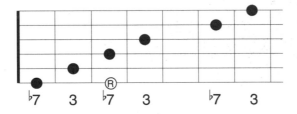

♭7   3   ♭7   3   ♭7   3

Tritones will form a nice symmetrical stair-step pattern on your guitar neck that is easy to remember. The step between the third and second strings is a little bigger (again, this is because of the guitar's tuning). The pattern starts a whole step below the root, on the ♭7.

PHOTO • ROBERT KNIGHT

Robert Cray

Here is an A Minor Pentatonic scale with the ♭7-3 pattern superimposed over the top of the scale. This will work over an A7 chord.

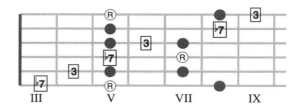

Here are some examples of resolving to ♭7 and 3 in A Minor Pentatonic.

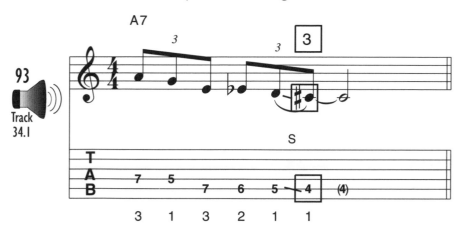

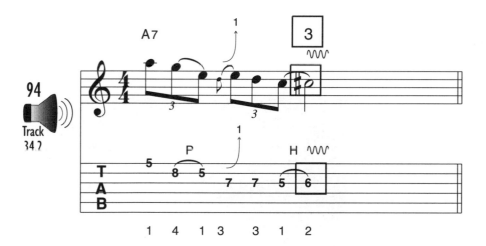

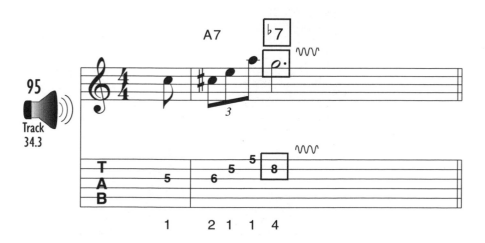

Here are the ♭7 and 3 tones in the key of A for I (A7), IV (D7) and V (E7) superimposed over the A Minor Pentatonic scale. Note that the tritone pattern always starts a whole step down from the root of the chord, on the ♭7.

3 and ♭7 for A7 in A Minor Pentatonic

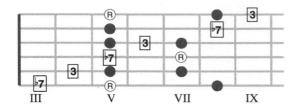

3 and ♭7 for D7 in A Minor Pentatonic

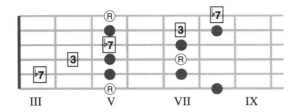

3 and ♭7 for E7 in A Minor Pentatonic

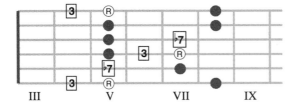

Bonnie Raitt

Here are two pentatonic licks in the key of A Minor demonstrating these resolutions over a IV chord (D7).

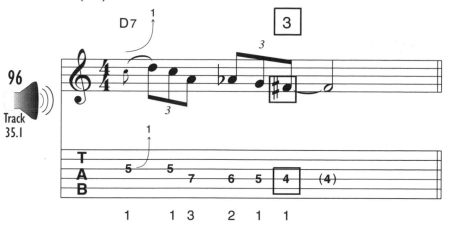

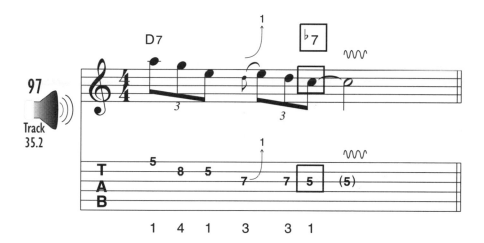

Here are two licks in A Minor Pentatonic demonstrating these resolutions over a V chord (E7).

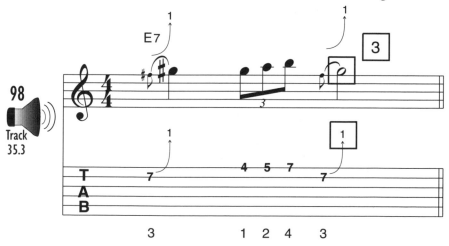

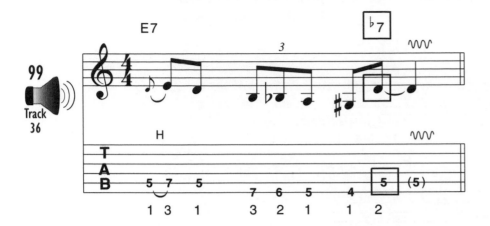

Get the idea? The great thing about the tritone, symmetrical relationship between the 3 and the ♭7 is that all you need to do to find these tones is find a root anywhere, on any string, and start the tritone pattern a whole step down.

Here is a diagram of a full neck A7 tritone pattern superimposed over the A Minor Pentatonic scale.

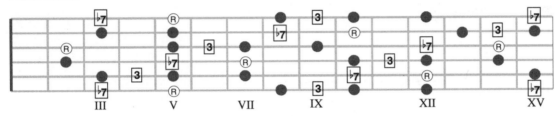

Still in the key of A, here is a full neck D7 tritone pattern superimposed over the A Minor Pentatonic scale.

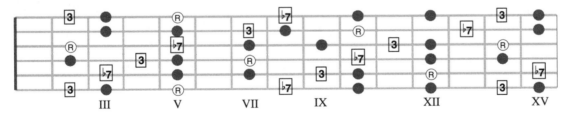

Here it is for a V chord (E7) in the key of A.

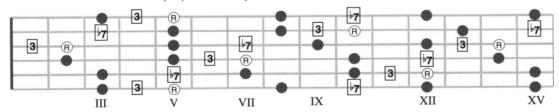

Remember to use these tones to end your phrases. This is a tool to add to your "bag of tricks." You don't *always* want to resolve to ♭7 and 3, as it will sound repetitious. Use your imagination!

DOUBLE-STOP 3RDS

Double-stops are two notes played together in a fill or a solo. Double-stop is just a very convenient way to say *harmonic interval*. In this section we will discuss double-stops and their applications for blues guitar. Double-stops are an absolutely essential part of any blues guitarists vocabulary. We will be discussing three kinds of double-stops: 1) 3rds; 2) 6ths (the same as 3rds, but inverted—see Chapter 2) and; 3) 4ths.

For these intervals to sound right in the key you are playing, they must be diatonic. That is to say that both of the notes in the double-stop have to be within the key, which is another way of saying "from the same major scale."

Let's start with 3rds. To find the diatonic 3rd for any note in a scale, simply skip up a note in the scale. Let's say we are using the key of D Major. In order to derive the 3rds from the scale you can do the following:

1) Write out the D major scale. To find the diatonic 3rd for the first note (D), simply skip over one note (E), and you will arrive at F#. You have found the 3rd of D: F#. It's that easy! If you do this for every note in the scale, you will get these results.

Now you have the 3rds for each note in the key.

An easier way of doing this is to remember the major key chord scale formula:

I	ii	iii	IV	V	vi	vii°
Maj	min	min	Maj	Maj	min	dim

Learning these simple, easy to remember interval patterns will complete the picture for you. If you know the major key chord scale formula and these interval patterns like the back of your hand, you can put them together to know what thirds to play, and on any string set.

3rds formed on the following string sets: sixth/fifth, fifth/fourth, fourth/third and second/first. The 3rds on all of these string sets have the following shapes:

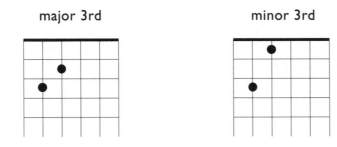

major 3rd   minor 3rd

3rds formed on the third string and second strings. Because of the way the third and second strings are tuned, a major 3rd apart, this will be different than the other string sets, which are tuned a perfect 4th apart.

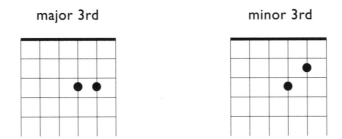

major 3rd   minor 3rd

If the chord scale shows a major chord, use a major 3rd. If the chord scale shows a minor or diminished chord, use a minor 3rd.

For the sake of easy communication let us agree to number each double-stop 3rd according to the number of the scale degree on the bottom. For instance, in the key of D the double-stop 3rd with an E on the bottom (E-G) will be called double-stop 2 since E is the second note of the D Major scale.

Here is how you would play through the 3rds in the key of D Major.

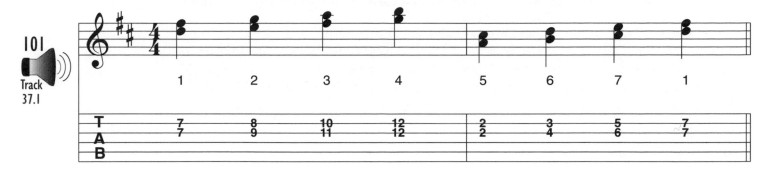

Here are 3rds in the key of G Major.

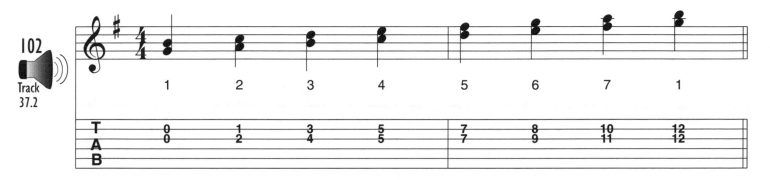

Here are 3rds in the key of A Major.

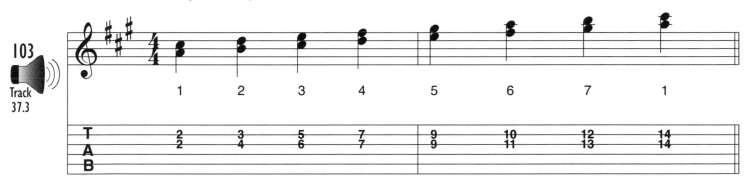

Usually, when playing a major blues, you are using dominant chords. That is why we often call it *dominant blues*. As we discussed earlier in the Funky Blues fills section of Chapter 3, dominant chords imply a V chord of a major key. So when playing an A7 chord, you can improvise with double-stops in the key of D Major, because A7 is the V chord in the key of D Major.

Here is an example of a double-stop solo in D over an A7 chord.

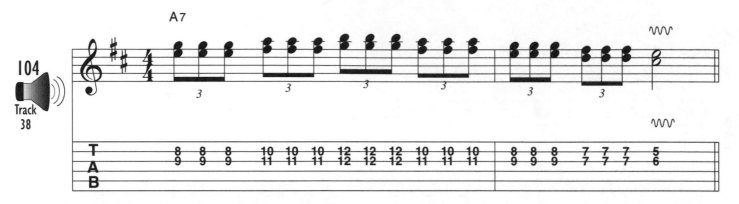

Sounds cool, doesn't it? Bet you've heard that kind of thing before! When you are playing double-stops in D over an A7 chord, try to resolve to the 2nd, 4th, 5th and 7th double-stop in the key of D. These double-stops contain notes in an A7 chord. You should use this as a rule of thumb: Always resolve to double-stops 2, 4, 5 or 7 of the key in which you are playing the double-stops.

So, in a blues in A, over A7, you would play double-stops in D Major. Resolve licks to double-stops 2 (E-G), 4 (G-B), 5 (A-C♯) or 7 (C♯-E) of D Major.

When you go to the IV chord in the key of A (D7), you would play double-stops in G Major (D7 is V in G Major). Over D7, resolve your licks to the double-stops 2 (A-C), 4 (C-E), 5 (D-F♯), or 7 (F♯-A) in the key of G, as these double-stops will include notes of a D7 chord.

When you hit the V chord in an A blues (E7), you would play double-stops in A Major (E7 is V in A Major). Once again, resolve to double-stops 2 (B-D), 4 (D-F♯), 5 (E-G♯), or 7 (G♯-B) of A Major, as they will include chord tones of an E7 chord.

If you are still confused, go back to the Funky Blues Fills section of Chapter 3. We did the same thing there, but using triads instead of double-stops. OK? OK! Here are the double-stops for an A blues. The resolution double-stops are shown in boxes.

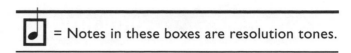 = Notes in these boxes are resolution tones.

Double-stops in D played over an A7 chord.

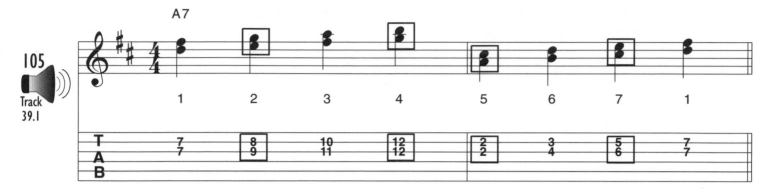

Double-stops in G played over a D7 chord.

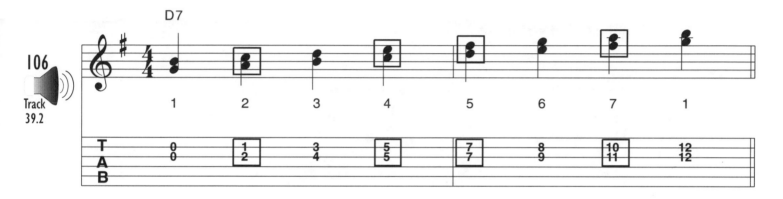

Double-stops in A played over an E7 chord.

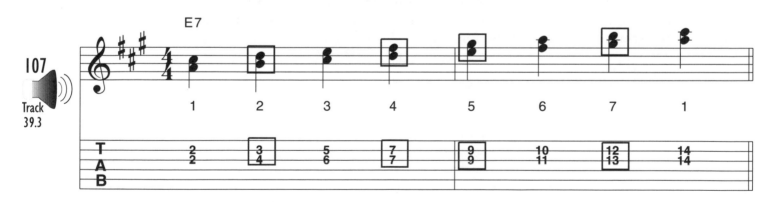

Dominant Blues Quiz. (Turn the book upside-down for the answers.)

A) Over an A7 chord, in what key would you play your double-stops?
B) How about over a C7 chord?
C) What about a B7 chord?
D) What about an F7 chord?

Answers: A) D, B) F, C) E, D) B♭

DOUBLE-STOP 6THS

If you fully understand the concept of dominant blues resolutions, you can try it with 6ths, which are the same as 3rds that have been inverted. To invert an interval simply means to turn it upside down. The tone that was on the bottom goes on top, or vice-versa (see Chapter 2 for a more thorough explanation).

6ths on the sixth/fourth, fifth/third and third/first string sets.

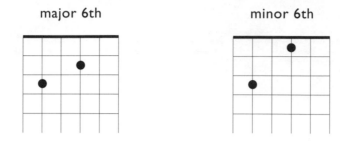

6ths on the fourth/second string set.

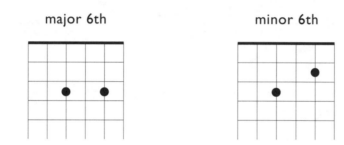

These should be applied in the same way we discussed the 3rds, except with 6ths you should resolve to double-stops 2, 4, 6, or 7 (instead of 2, 4, 5, and 7 as with 3rds). Try some of the examples for 3rds using 6ths instead.

Here are two licks using 6ths in D Major over an A7 chord.

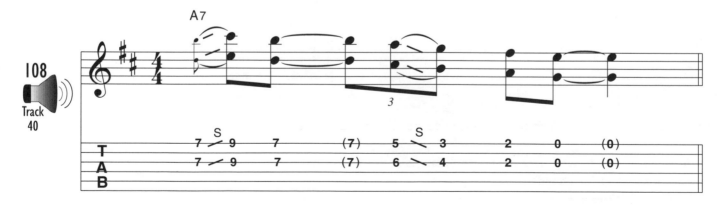

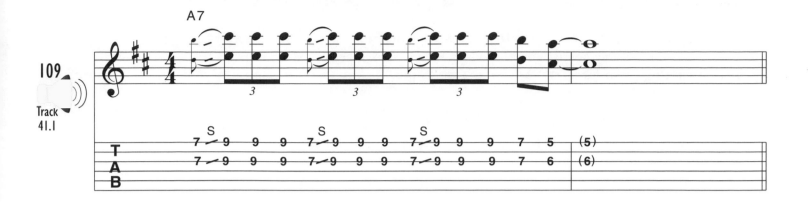

Here are two licks using 6ths, or inverted 3rds, in G Major over a D7 chord.

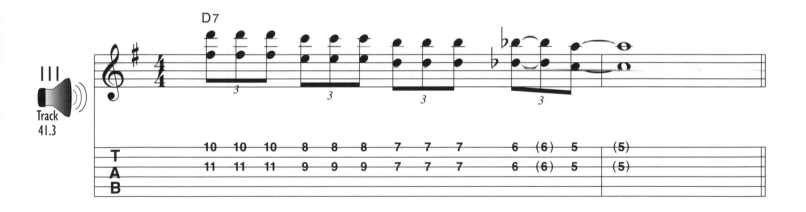

DOUBLE-STOP 4THS

One of my favorite things to do is to play double-stop 4ths (which are the same as inverted 5ths). This is commonly heard in bluesy ballads and Hendrix, Curtis Mayfield inspired R & B. There are only two forms to learn so let's get to them.

4ths on the sixth/fifth, fifth/fourth, fourth/third, and second/first string sets will all have this shape.

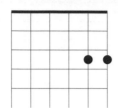

4ths on the third/second string set have a different shape.

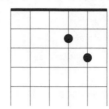

When you are in a major key, playing a beautiful ballad, base these double-stops on the major pentatonic scale: 1, 2, 3, 5, and 6 of the major scale (see Chapter 5).

Here is an exercise using 4hs over a simple I - IV progression in G Major.

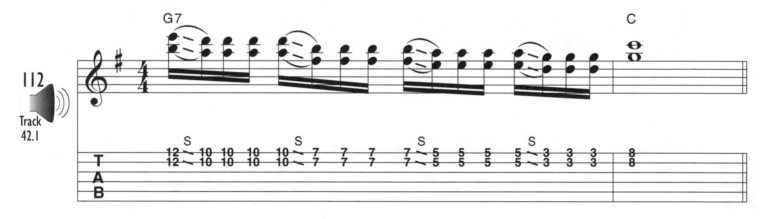

These double-stops also sound beautiful when combined with the R & B, Hendrix-style rhythms we examined earlier in the book. Here is an example combining both over a C to F Major progression.

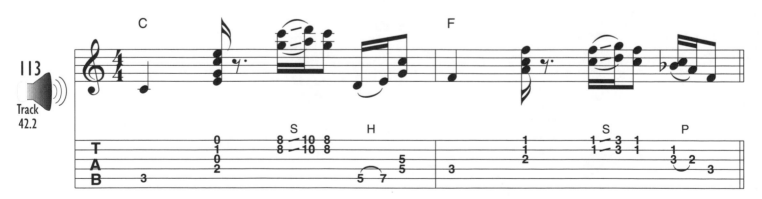

When in minor keys, base the 4th double-stops on the minor pentatonic scale: 1, ♭3, 4, 5, and ♭7. Here is an example using double-stops over an Amin7 chord.

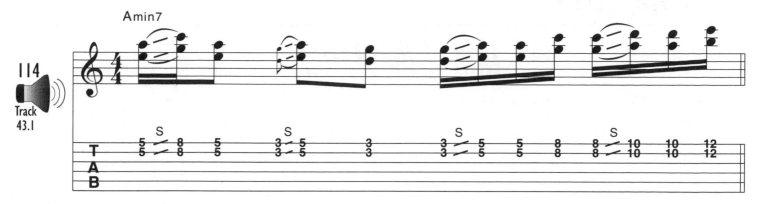

Here is one for an Amin7 to Dmin7 progression.

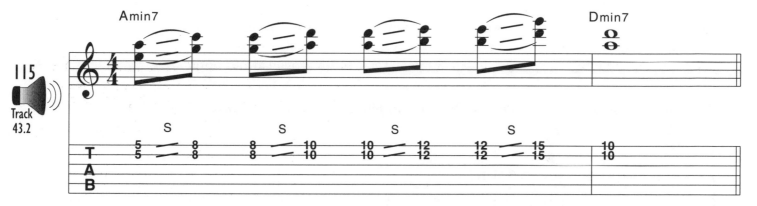

MINOR BLUES DOUBLE-STOPS

For minor blues, you should play the double-stops from the relative major key. The root of the relative major key can be found three frets up from the root of the minor chord (see Chapter 2 to read more about relative minor and major keys). Over an A Minor blues, you would play double-stops in C Major throughout the progression—over the i, iv and v chords.

Minor Blues Quiz. (Turn book upside-down for answers.)

A) Over a minor blues in E, in what major key would you play your double-stops?
B) Over a minor blues in D, in what major key would you play your double-stops?
C) How about a C Minor blues?
D) F Minor blues?

Answers: A) G, B) F, C) E♭, D) A♭

CHAPTER 7

Licks of the Masters

Here it is, the meat and potatoes, the center of the biscuit, the moment we have been waiting for, a veritable feast of licks and techniques by some of the finest blues guitarists who have ever laid fingers on the fretboard! We start with the three Kings, B. B., Albert and Freddie.

B. B. KING

For me, the true king of the blues will always be B. B. King. Not just for his incredible guitar playing, but also for his showmanship, his voice and his warm-hearted, giving attitude towards his fans. We can all learn a lot from B. B. The following diagram represents B.B.'s approach to integrating major and minor pentatonic scales around a root note.

B.B. King's Approach to Integrating Major and Minor Pentatonic Scales

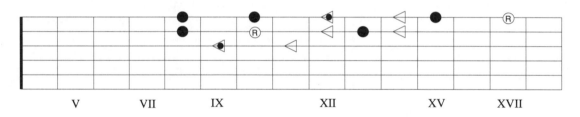

® = Root
◁ = Major Pentatonic
● = Minor Pentatonic
◀ = Major and Minor Pentatonic

In the following examples you'll notice how B. B. tends to resolve his licks to the root of the key, in this case A. Sometimes B. B. will also resolve to the major 3rd of the key, in this case C♯. He will occasionally resolve to the ♭7, as well. Here are some licks in the style of B. B. King.

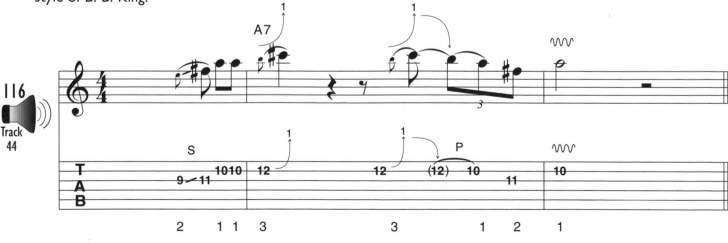

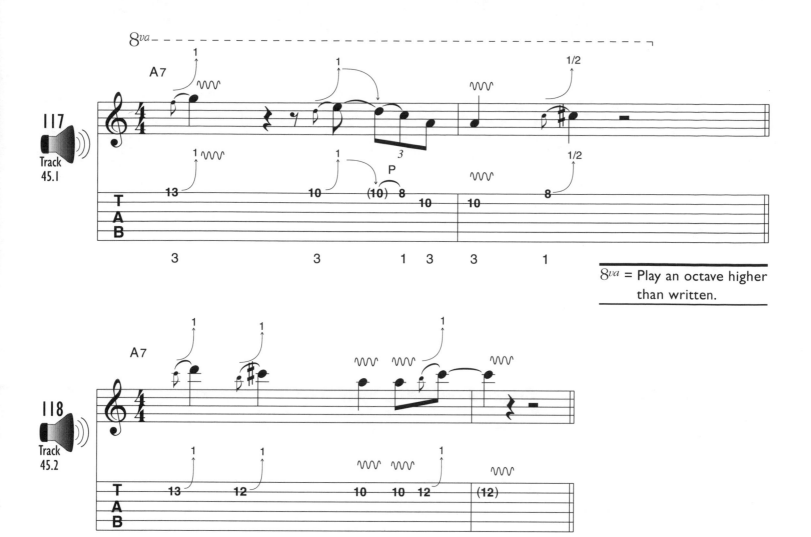

8va = Play an octave higher than written.

Here are some licks showing how B. B. might approach an A Minor blues.

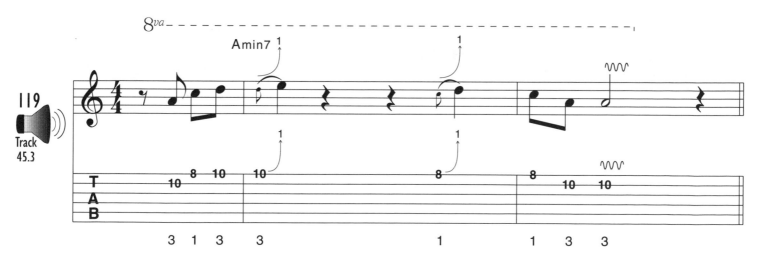

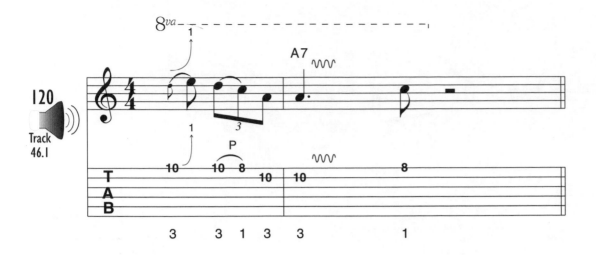

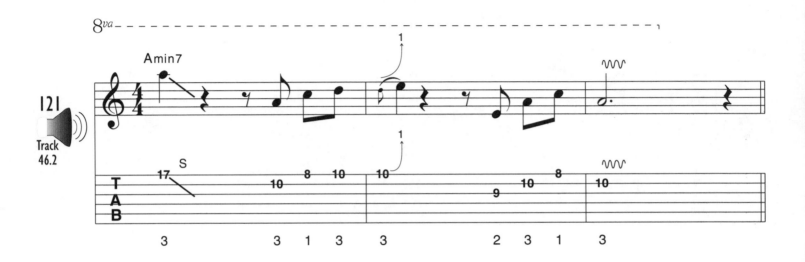

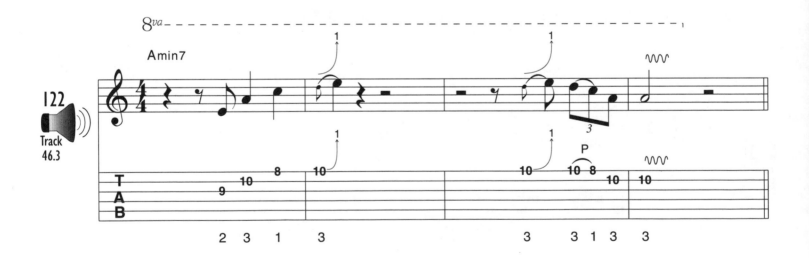

Make sure you try to relate the licks in Examples 116-122 to the B.B. King scale diagram on page 88. It will help you understand how these licks are built.

ALBERT KING

Albert King has influenced countless guitarists from Jimi Hendrix to Stevie Ray Vaughn to Buddy Guy. He is the master of the wide bend and the composer of such classics as "Crosscut Saw" and "Born Under a Bad Sign." Wielding his trademark flying V, "Lucy," Albert King played like no one else. These example licks are in the key of A Major.

Notice the impact Albert has had on modern bluesmen such as Stevie Ray Vaughan. You could hear the bending style in Stevie's playing. Albert King has since passed on, but his sound, soul and style will live on in the generations of blues guitarists he has influenced.

FREDDIE KING

Freddie King was nicknamed the "Texas Cannonball" for his fiery, intense guitar playing, and his gritty, soulful singing. Influenced by Lightnin' Hopkins, Muddy Waters, B. B. and T- Bone Walker, Freddie also brought elements of rock guitar playing into his own style. Freddie composed the blues standard "Hideaway" which has been covered by Eric Clapton, among others. Although Freddie passed away in 1976, he lives on in our memories forever. Here are some examples in the style of Freddie King.

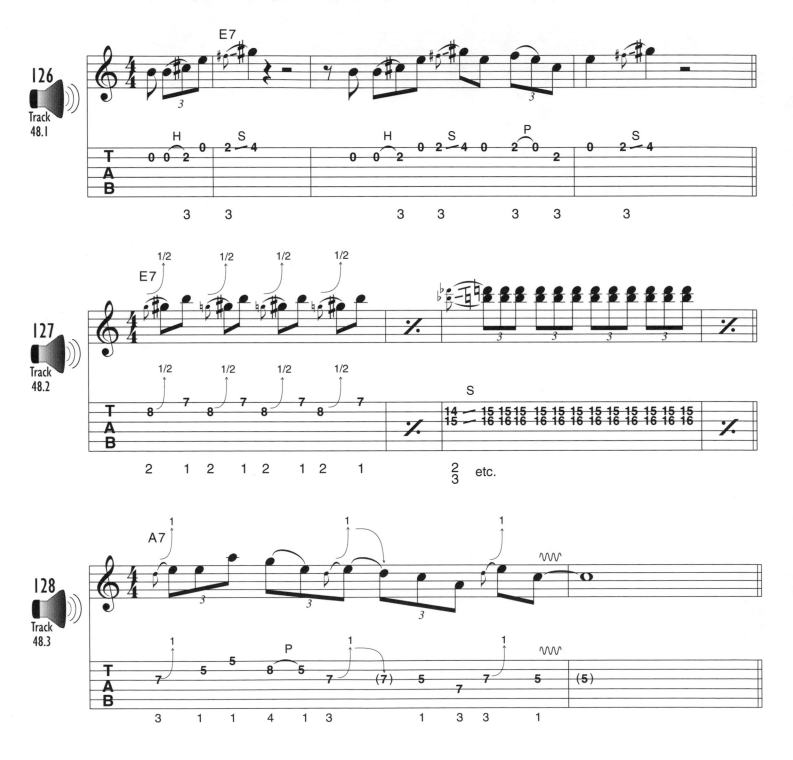

JIMI HENDRIX

Jimi Hendrix is considered to be the greatest rock guitar player of all time, but he thought of himself as a blues man. Just one listen to "Red House" on *Killin' Floor* shows Jimi's roots. Jimi opened the gates for a flood of blues/rock guitarists, all of whom were directly influenced by him. Here are some examples of fine blues playing in the style of Jimi Hendrix.

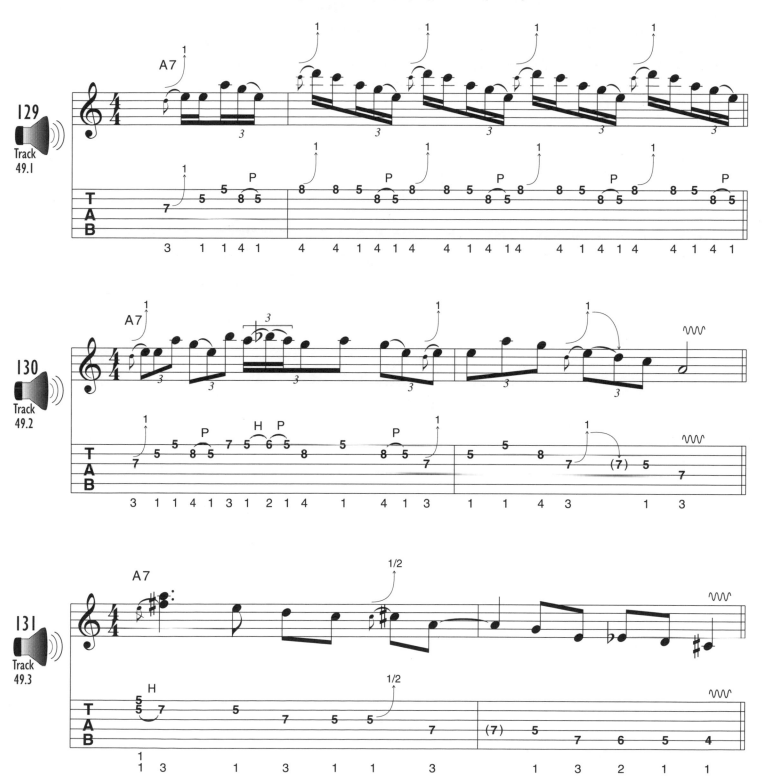

ERIC CLAPTON

England has long been the breeding ground of many great blues/rock guitarists. A stunning young blues guitarist emerged from the Yardbirds and John Mayall's Blues Breakers. "Clapton is God" began appearing as mysterious graffiti all over London. Then came Cream and the world came to learn about Eric Clapton as the leader of Europe's blues guitarists.

Though known mainly for his rock guitar playing, Eric plays the blues with the love and conviction of a true devotee. All of his albums have at least one blues tune. Eric has covered songs by Willie Dixon, Robert Johnson and Freddie King, among others. Here are some approaches Eric Clapton would use over a blues in A Major.

STEVIE RAY VAUGHAN

The most influential of modern blues guitarists would have to be Austin, Texas's favorite son, Stevie Ray Vaughan. Although he passed on at an early age, he's still studied and worshipped as no other guitarist since Hendrix. Taking influences as diverse as Albert King and Jimi Hendrix, Stevie had the rare gift of an instantly identifiable sound. There was no mistaking his touch. Here are some signature licks that Stevie would use over an A Major blues.

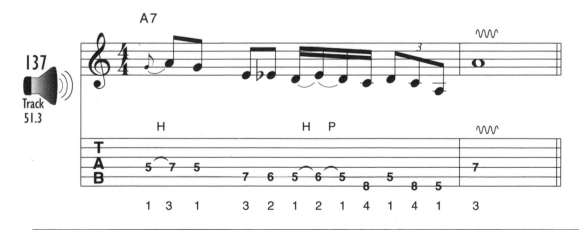